In Loving Memory

Gravestone Inscriptions and Memorials
in
East Hoathly Churchyard

Compiled and edited by

Jane Seabrook

ISBN 0 9524516 3 8

Also published by CTR Publishing:
The Diary of Thomas Turner
Edited by David Vaisey
As Clean a Lot of Children as He Had Ever Seen
Edited by Jane Seabrook

Computer Mapping by Richard Spencer, Eastbourne, East Sussex

Typeset by David Brown, Maynards Green, East Sussex.

Printed by Windmill Press, Hadlow, Down, East Sussex.

In Loving Memory

Kind reader stay and shed a tear
And shew the dust that lieth here
His glass is run, his breath is spent
His days are gone, his life was lent

Compiled and edited by
Jane Seabrook.

CTR Publishing,
9 High Street,
East Hoathly,
Nr. Lewes,
East Sussex.

1999

CONTENTS

FOREWORD

As far as I am aware there has never been a detailed map of East Hoathly Churchyard, which has made it very hard to find long lost relatives on receipt of enquiries.

So to this end I am deeply grateful to Jane Seabrook, our local amateur historian, for taking this task on board. Helped by Bob, her husband, and Eric Gould, the Church's Verger, she has plotted, scraped and crawled around the memorials, learning a bit of history here and there, and seeing who was connected with whom.

Too much of our local history is being lost, so hopefully this book will preserve this information for many generations to come.

Thank you, Jane, and I hope that you have received as much from this project as you have given.

Peter Clark,
The Rectory,
East Hoathly.
May 1999

ACKNOWLEDGEMENTS

Firstly, I must thank the Rev. Peter Clark for deciding he would like a map of the graves in the churchyard so that he could answer queries from visitors searching for their ancestors. Thanks to Peter Clerehugh for suggesting that I took on the task; special thanks to Eric Gould for his knowledge and for helping in minor excavations to reveal inscriptions. Thanks to Richard Spencer for the mapping, mostly from my atrociously badly drawn maps on scraps of paper, and thanks to those who lent me books on churchyards, memorials, etc.

It has been a very interesting exercise and I hope the information will prove useful, if only in deciding to whom your Uncle Fred was married!

There are several puzzling burials which have been revealed and to which I can find no answer. For example, why is the plaque to Phoebe Turner on the grave for Louisa Thatcher? There seems to be no connection.

The churchyard is still in use, but the collection of inscriptions had, of course, to end sometime in order for the book to be published. They are complete to the end of April 1999. There will be, from time to time, an updated leaflet which can be included in the booklet.

Jane Seabrook

May 1999

Because of a delay in printing this book, it has been possible to add a few new inscriptions – see Appendix

July 1999.

View of East Hoathly Church, showing the Church Marks fence before the lychgate was built.

INTRODUCTION

The boundary of East Hoathly churchyard was once marked by a wooden post and rail fence, the upkeep of which was the responsibility of the parish landowners. This fence can be seen in the postcard reproduced on page xviii. The length of each section of fence was decided by the amount of land owned and the owner's initials were carved into the posts. Hence the name to-day of the adjacent lane – Church Marks Lane. It is recorded in 1726 that the Rev. Thomas Porter was responsible for three sections of fence, one of 8', one of 8½' and one of 10', and Hannah Atkins was responsible for 8' of fence. There is still a section of fence to be found in the middle of some hedge at the east end of the churchyard.

There is a great deal of superstition, some of pagan origin surrounding churchyards and burials. It is a general rule that the deceased was buried on an east to west orientation so that on the day of judgement he would rise facing the east; and the gravestones were generally carved so that the worshippers would see the inscription on their way in to church, and the least favoured area for burial was the north side. The oldest stones are the thickest. At East Hoathly the one for Richard Marchant is probably the thickest and this is dated 1757. For some reason there is No. 1 carved on the reverse.

Grave markers, as with most other things in this world, go through fashion changes. Early graves were marked with a simple wooden cross and an early eighteenth century wooden grave marker was the grave board, which is two posts with a connecting plank upon which was either carved or painted details of the deceased. One such grave board can be seen in the post card reproduced on the page 68. To the left of this board is a white round marker. This is a cast iron marker which could be ordered in the 1890's with the name of the deceased and the date of death at a cost of 3s. 9d. delivered to Uckfield Station. The Rector at the time, the Rev. Harbord, gave permission for them to be placed on the grave free of charge. There are only three of these markers in East Hoathly churchyard, and they appear to have strayed from their original places.

Seventeenth and eighteenth century headstones can be elaborate in their decorations, and are usually carved with symbols of mortality such as death's heads, an hourglass or a coffin. Some are decorated with angels blowing trumpets. (I have not attempted to describe all the headstones).

East Hoathly has several table or altar tombs, which were popular with the gentry and they were sometimes surrounded by iron grilles or railings, which were removed during the 2nd World War for scrap.

In Victorian times the gentry had ornate memorials - the one to the Rickett family being the most elaborate.

The Industrial Revolution brought mass production and introduced standardised patterns and designs for memorials, so individuality was gradually lost, and uniformity became the norm. There also appears to be a standardisation of quotations, particularly in recent years. One particular quotation is used no less than seven times from 1951 to 1968.

Some biblical quotations from the Victorian gravestones can be puzzling as they do not appear to make too much sense, but presumably they are taken from the deceased's favourite part of the Bible.

There is one further type of gravestone which needs to be mentioned, and that is the ledger. This is a large flat rectangular slab inset into the ground, usually inside the church. East Hoathly has three - one just in front of the inside door of the tower to John Mittel, a further one which is underneath the carpet in the bell tower. This is very worn, but I believe it to be to Timothy Parker. There is a further ledger which is leaning against the outside east wall. This was removed from inside the church during renovation work, and it is to the Rev. Haworth.

And lastly, a mention of the Harmer panels in the headstones Nos. F204 and F240. Jonathan Harmer lived in Heathfield and was the son of a stonemason. Jonathan specialised in these terra-cotta bas-reliefs which can be found in other churchyards in the Heathfield area. There is a modern copy in the headstone No. H498. This was commissioned by the family of Shirley Harrison and made by Peartree Pottery which used to trade from the Old Chapel in the High Street in East Hoathly.

There is one inscription which has been taken from the postcard reproduced on page 34. It is on a wooden cross and plaque to Margaret Whapham which is to the right of the cross with the rope surround.

When planning this book, I had intended that all inscriptions should be reproduced in the form they appear on the headstones and kerbs, but I soon discovered that inscriptions which are on the kerbs are very long, and they would not fit onto the printed page! The layout of these has therefore been altered to fit the space available, and are not as seen on the memorial. A few headstones are very worn and unreadable parts are indicated by square brackets [ ]. The information in some of these square brackets is based on information taken from the Parish burial register.

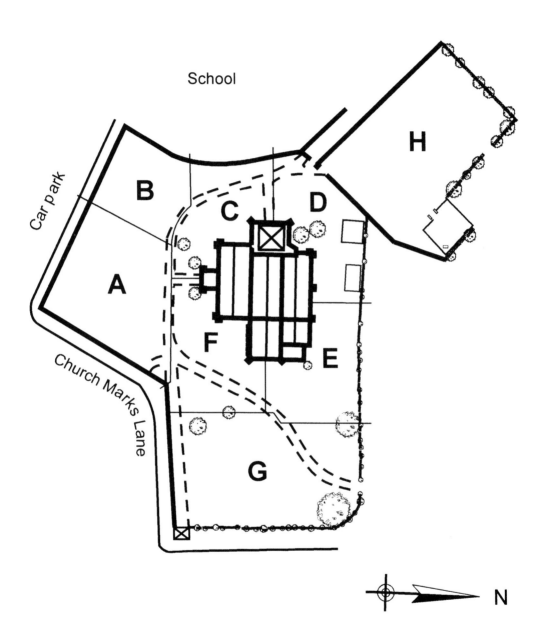

School

Car park

Church Marks Lane

A

B

C

D

E

F

G

H

N

SECTION A

SECTION A
A1 – 86

A1

Red granite
headstone and
kerb

In loving memory of
a dearly loved husband and father
Ernest Alexander Jones
called to higher service 14th April 1946
aged 77 years
He was headmaster of East Hoathly School from
1896 to 1930, and the last 50 years of his life
were devoted to the welfare of this village
"Well done, good and faithful servant"
and of his wife
Alice Elizabeth
5th May 1870 – 14th March 1958
*"Then are they glad because they are at
rest and so he bringeth them unto the
haven where they would be"*

A2

Kerb

To the cherished memory of
F. E. Holmes, who died 27th Dec. 1936
Also of her husband, **Walter Holmes**
who died 28th January 1962 aged 73 years

A3

Kerb

In loving memory of **Sophia Sarah Hannay**
Born April 27th 1847, died July 26th 1928
Hold thou me up and I shall be safe

A4

Kerb

Ever loving memory of our dear boy, **Eric Lloyd Duly**
Born Sept. 12 1910   died June 6th 1928
Also of **Edith Alicia**, his dear sister
who died Feb. 10th 1933 aged 17
"Resting"
On the great day in the distance

A5

Headstone

In
loving remembrance
of
Rebecca
the beloved wife of
Benjamin Cottington
who entered into rest
on May 22 1926, aged 55 years
Poor and afflicted Lord are thine
she joined the bright celestial throng
her sufferings now have reached a close
and heaven afford her sweet repose
No cloud shall now destruct her sun
but all is life and peace

A6

Red granite block
(rough hewn) and
kerb

In
loving memory of
Hannah
the beloved wife of
William Parris
Died October 17th 1925, aged 62
For ever with the Lord
Also of
William Parris
Died April 3 1940, aged 78
Foot stone: *Thy will be done*

A7

Headstone

In
loving memory
of
John Henry Reed, who died Dec. 5th 1919
aged 77 years
In every state search kept as Jehovah's eye,
'tis well with them while life endure
and well when called to die
Also of **Sarah Reed**
wife of the above
who died Feb. 19th 1922
aged 83 years
At rest

A8

Cross and kerb

In loving memory
of
Arthur William Chalmers Peskett
M.A., M.B., B.C. Cantab
born Simla, India 23rd Aug. 1857
Died at "Simla", Halland 22nd Nov. 1912
aged 55 years
Also of **Edith Jane** wife of the above
who died 29th March 1925
aged 86 years.
Also of 2nd Lieut. **C. E. H. Peskett**
4th Batt: Duke of Wellington's W. Riding Regt.
Killed in action 3rd May 1917, aged 28 years
Also of
Enid Blanche Peskett who died 19th Feb. 1927
aged 34 years
"Where beyond those voices there is peace"

A9

Headstone and
footstone

Beloved and loving parents
In
loving memory
of
Edmund Parris
who died 15th May 1908
aged 75 years
*"He that endureth to the end shall
be saved" Matt. X.22
Dear dying lamb! Thy precious blood
shall never lose its power
'till all the ransom'd Church of God
be saved to sin no more*
Also of **Hannah**
beloved wife of the above
who died 5th January 1920
aged 84 years
"With Christ, which is far better" Phil: 1.23
(Foot stone: E.P. 1908   H.P. 1920)

4

A10

Headstone and
footstone

In memory of
Rosina Eliza
the beloved wife of
Ebenezer Hall
of this Parish
who died 2nd May 1908
aged 27 years
Till we meet again
It is not exile, rest on high
It is not sadness, peace from strife
To fall asleep is not to die
To dwell with Christ is better life"
(Foot stone: R.E.H. 1908)

A11

Headstone

In loving memory
of
Walter Kemp
late of Crouch's Farm
in this Parish
Born 1st January 1841
Died 29th January 1898
"Father, not my will, but thine be done!"
Also of **Elizabeth**
the beloved wife of the above
Born 8th December 1843
Died 17th August 1923
"Thou shalt guide me with thy counsel and
afterward receive me to glory"

A12

Cross on
3-tiered
plinth with
kerb

In loving memory
of
Mabel Colgate Holman
who died 29th May 1897
aged 26 years
In loving memory
of
Jane Meade Holman
wife of
Henry Colgate Holman
Born 18th Feby. 1839 died 23rd April 1923
In loving memory
of
Henry Colgate Holman
Born 10th Nov. 1832
Died 13th April 1912
Edith Mary Holman who died 10th December 1946
Thou wilt keep him in perfect peace,
whose mind is stayed on Thee because
he trusteth in Thee. Isaiah XXVI. 3

A13

Cross on
3-tiered
plinth with
kerb

In loving memory of
Frederick Thomas Jones
Born 12th October 1865
Died 29th April 1896
Into thy hands I commend my spirit
Erected by his relatives and friends
Also by the Managers, teachers and
children of the National School in the
Parish of which he was the head master
for five years
Caroline Jones
Sept. 25th 1841
Dec. 8th 1924
in the certain hope
of a glorious resurrection
and joyful recognition
For sixty years the best of wives
a loving mother
excellent teacher, noble example
In loving
memory of
Alice Alexandra Jones
"Cissie"
born 13th march 1903
Died 27th November 1911
"Safely, Safely gather'd in,
far from sorrow, far from sin,
God has saved from weary strife,
in its dawn this fresh young life,
now it waits for us above,
resting in
the saviour's love"
Also in loving memory of **Frederick Jones**
Born 29th March 1842 Died 21st March 1931
60 years a zealous worker for his Church, School and parish

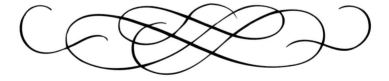

A14

Headstone and
footstone

In loving memory
of **Ann Novis**
the beloved wife of
Thomas Novis
who departed this life 22nd May 1894
aged 72 years
"For a small moment have I forsaken thee
but with great mercies will I gather thee" Isaiah: LIV.7
Also
Thomas Novis
the beloved husband of
Ann Novis
who departed this life 6th Sept. 1898
aged 78 years
Their end was peace
in a little wrath I hid my face from thee
for a moment, but with everlasting kindness
will I have mercy on thee saith the Lord
Thy redeemer Isaiah: LIV 8
(Foot stone: A.N. 1894   T.N. 1898)

⋅⇒———————⇐⋅

A15

Kerb

In loving memory of
David Mannering of Halland
who entered into rest September 6th 1918 aged 82 years
"Who waits for thy salvation Lord
shall thy salvation see"
Also in fond memory of **Kezia Penelope**, wife of David Mannering
who fell asleep February 28th 1929 aged 83 years
"In thy presence is fullness of joy"

⋅⇒———————⇐⋅

A16

Headstone

In loving memory of
Eliza Kate Streeter
who died June 10th 1892
aged 43 years
"Unto you therefore which believe he
is precious" I Peter: II. 7
Also of her second daughter
Lilian Maude Streeter
who died December 29th 1968
aged 92 years

A17

Small plaque

In
loving memory
of **Trayton Baldock**
15th March 1942
aged 76

A18

Open book

In loving
memory of
George Ralph
Died Nov. 7th
1941
aged 62 years

Also **Harriett**
his wife
Died Nov. 29th
1946 aged 64 years
At rest

A19

Plain cross
with kerb

In memory of
Louisa Stickland
who died in this Parish, Mar. 8 1892
aged 70
Blessed are they that hear the word of God"

A20

Headstone
with kerb

In
loving memory
of
David Leslie
the much loved eldest son of
David and Penelope Mannering
who fell asleep in Jesus June 26th 1912
Aged 35 years
"The Lord is my shepherd I shall not want" *Psalm 3.1*
Each feeble soul by him enrolled
under one shepherd in one fold
Shut in, they shall go out no more
Also of **Maude**
the beloved second daughter of the above
who entered into rest November 29th 1915
aged 42 years
"With Christ, which is far better
Underneath are the everlasting arms"
Also of **Bertha Mary**
the beloved eldest daughter of the above
who fell asleep in Christ December 6th 1916
aged 47 years
"In my father's house are many mansions"
"For ever with the Lord"

A21

Red granite
sarcophagus,
railings missing

In memory of
Mary the dearly-loved and loving wife
of George David Jones, Barrister of the Inner Temple
Born August 4th 1824, fell asleep June 14th 1894
Now sweetly sleep; Angels thy soul receive
and bear to Jesus' breast
Long in our hearts thy memory shall live; here let thy body rest,
secure from earthly pain and sorrow,
till dawns the resurrection morrow;
now sweetly sleep; "I am the resurrection and the life"
John XI.25
In loving memory of
George David Jones of Hove, Sussex, Barrister
and Minister of Ebenezer Chapel, Tonbridge,
who peacefully fell asleep in Jesus on Dec. 2nd 1910,
in his 90th year
Also of **Caroline Shorter**, his sister-in-law,
who entered into rest on Dec. 10th 1910 aged 79 years
With God

A22

Headstone
with kerb

In
loving memory
of
Alfred Gifkins
who died 21st June 1913
in the 73rd year of his age
At rest
And of **Jane** his loving wife
who fell asleep 14th March 1925
aged 89 years
Then are they glad because they are at
rest, and so he bringeth them unto the
haven where they would be

A23

Cross with
kerb

In memory of
Sylvia May
the dearly
loved daughter of
Thomas and Sylvia Holman
Died February 18th 1902
aged 26 years
And they shall be mine saith the Lord of hosts
in that day when I make up my jewels. Mal. III. 17
Also of
Thomas Holman
Surgeon in this Parish
for 49 years
Died October 23rd 1909
aged 71 years
Also of
Sylvia
wife of Thomas Holman
Died February 17th 1929
aged 83 years

A24

Headstone
and kerb

In loving memory of
Susan
the dearly beloved wife of
George David Hall
Born May 6th 1863
Died March 24th 1904
When I awake up after thy likeness I
shall be satisfied with it"

A25

Headstone

In loving memory
of
William George
fourth son of
Walter Luther and Fanny Kemp
of Crouch's Farm, in this Parish
who died of wounds received in action
30th October 1918
aged 20 years
Greater love hath no man than this,
that he lay down his life
for his King and country
Also of **Walter Luther Kemp**,
father of the above
Died 5th March 1952
aged 86 years
Resting

A26

Headstone
and kerb

In
ever loving memory
of
George Corke Eade
of Hesmonds Farm, East Hoathly
who died August 16th 1919
aged 48 years
"When thou passest through the
waters, I will be with thee
and through the rivers they
shall not overflow thee"
And of
Kate Harriet Eade
his beloved wife
1872-1955

A27

Kerb

In loving memory of
Julia, the beloved wife of George Henry Trill,
died 29th June 1926 aged 66 years
Also of **George Henry Trill**
died 28th November 1943 aged 82 years
Resting

A28

Marble
surround

In loving memory of my devoted husband
George Reginald Trill who died 28th Decr 1929 aged 40 years
Waiting

A28P*

Flower holder

In loving memory
of
Reginald
and
Blanche
Trill

* Note – Blanche Trill died on 5th January 1977 aged 85 and her ashes are buried at The Park Crematorium, Aldershot. She was the wife of George Reginald Trill.

A29

Kerb with
headstone

In loving memory of
Emily Hannah
Goldsmith
who died Nov. 14th 1937
aged 56 years
wife of George Thomas Goldsmith
who was killed in action at Arras 1917

A30

Kerb

In loving memory of
Alexander Stewart, died December 4th 1936 aged 63 years
Also of his wife
Jean Stewart Died October 2nd 1956 aged 79 years

A30PA

Plaque

In loving memory of
Jean Stewart
Died 25th March 1982
aged 75 years

A31

Kerb

In loving memory of
Harriet Ruth, the beloved wife of David William Trill
who died 8th December 1930 aged 62 years
Also of **David William Trill**
who died 16th December 1955 aged 87 years
At rest

A32

Headstone

In
loving memory
of
my dear husband
Edward Streeter
who passed to his rest
12th March 1929
aged 76
"Blessed is the man that feareth the Lord"
Also of
Sarah Jane
the beloved wife of the above
who passed away 22nd May 1939
aged 81 years

A32PA

Plaque

**Katharine
Maud Brewis**
neé Cain
24 – 6 – 1910 19 – 12 – 1993
wife of Rev. Noel R. Brewis
Granddaughter of Edward Streeter
Missionary nurse to India
*A true Christian lady
and wise gentle mother
who spent her life
caring for others*

A33

Cross and kerb

In
loving memory
of
James Partridge
Died March 4th 1909
aged 43 years
In
loving memory
of
Lilian Mary Partridge
Died March 24th 1925
aged 61 years
Also of
William Partridge
Died October 29th 1928
aged 39 years

———

A34

Headstone
and kerb

In loving memory
of
Mark Bristow
for more than 50 years a carrier
from this village to Brighton
who died 23rd June 1925
aged 75 years
"God shall wipe away all tears from their eyes" *Rev. XXI. 4*
Also of
Emma his third wife
who passed away 8th Decr. 1919
Patient in suffering

———

A35

Headstone

In loving memory
of
James William Burt
who died 12th April 1919
aged 74 years
Also of
Emily
wife of the above
who passed away 28th Feb. 1926
aged 72 years
At rest

A36

Kerb

In loving memory
Jane Arkell a sister of D. Arkell
fell asleep 7th Feby 1918 aged 78 years
Daniel Arkell with Christ 29th October 1923 in his 75th year
Mary Susan beloved wife of Daniel Arkell
passed to her rest 3rd Novr. 1932 aged 93 years

⊷══──────────══⊶

A37

Headstone
with kerb

In
loving memory
of
Emily Minnie Rich
who died Sept. 1st 1904
aged 27 years
"So He giveth His beloved sleep"
Also of
William Andrew Rich
brother of the above
who died Sept. 21st 1938
aged 63 years
"Ye know not the day nor the hour"

⊷══──────────══⊶

A38

Cross and kerb

Jesu
In loving memory
of
Louisa Dorothy Foster
born April 1st 1834
Died February 12th 1898
God in love

⊷══──────────══⊶

A39

Headstone

In loving remembrance
of
Edward Hoath
who died July 17th 1892
aged 24 years
*We have to mourn the loss of one
we did our best to save
beloved on earth regretted gone
remembered in the grave*
Also of **Ernest Hoath**
who died May 26th 1894
aged 20 years

A40

Kerb

In memory of
Mary Ann Brooker September 23rd 1941 aged 73 years
Resting

A41

Granite headstone

In
memory of our
dear mother
Annie Woodhams
Died 25th Nov. 1964
aged 87 years
Love's last gift - remembrance

A42

Headstone – cross
with rope border

In loving
memory of
Caroline Elizabeth
the beloved wife of
Alfred Henry Ellis
who died August 8th 1892
aged 23 years
"What I do thou knowest not now
but thou shalt know hereafter" John XIII. 7

A43*

Margaret Whapham
aged 61
Died 7th September 1926

* Note – The inscription to A43 has been taken from an old postcard (see page 34**)**. The grave was marked with a large plain wooden cross, with a central diamond shaped plaque all of which has long since disintegrated.

A44

Headstone
with kerb

In loving memory
of
our dear mother and father
Rose Beal
Died 23rd March 1945
aged 82 years
Robert Beal
Died 23rd January 1946
aged 83 years

A44PA*

Plaque

George David Beal
Died Sept. 2nd 1961
aged 64 years
At rest

★ Note – **George David Beal** was the son of Rose and Robert.

A45

Headstone

In
loving memory
of
Sarah Parris
who departed this life 14th May 1906
aged 66 years
"Patient in suffering"
Also of
Robert Parris
husband of the above
who died 14th January 1915
aged 82 years
"At rest"

A46

Headstone
and kerb

In
loving memory
of
William Wenham
who died Novr. 22nd 1909
aged 71 years
Also of
Mary his wife
who died Decr. 30th 1909
aged 67 years
"He giveth His beloved sleep"

19

A47

Headstone

In
loving memory
of
Andrew Francis Rich
who died 19th July 1919
aged 67
At rest
Also of
Maria Ann
his wife
who died 7th Sept. 1927
aged 73
At Peace

———————————

A48

Kerb and
3-tiered plinth
(top missing)

In
loving memory of
Ronnie (Laddie)
only child of
Edith & late Edward Morley
Died July 28th 1919
aged 3 years 4 months
Lost awhile our treasured love
gained for ever safe above

———————————

A49

Cross with
3-tiered plinth

In
loving memory of
my dear husband
George William Lindsay
late Royal Canadian Horse Artillery
who died April 4th 1920
aged 28 years
His sweet life to us was only lent
his work is done and victory won
In loving
memory of
a dear brother
William George Carley
late 4th Middlesex Regt
killed in action at Arras
April 23rd 1917
He is reaping his reward
and is at rest

A50

Granite cross on
rough hewn base

In loving memory of our dear son
Charles Edward Buckett
who fell asleep Feb. 6th 1927
aged 16 years
The Lord gave and the Lord hath taken away
Also in ever loving memory of
Tamar Buckett
mother of the above
Died June 26th 1947
aged 74 years
Also
in dear memory of
**Charles David
Buckett**
Died June 23rd 1951
aged 78 years

A51

Cross with
3-tiered plinth

In loving memory
of
Caroline Laura Morley
Died April 16th 1931
aged 83 years
Peace, perfect peace
Also of **William Morley**
Died April 16th 1932 aged 83 years
Peace perfect peace

A52

Headstone

In loving memory
Alfred Finch
Died Oct 12 1933 aged 78
and his wife
Fanny Finch
Died Dec. 8 1941 aged 87
their daughter
Olive Hutson
Died April 25 1968 aged 79
and her husband
Percy Blishen Hutson
Died April 14th 1970 aged 89
and their son
John Blishen Hutson
Died Feb. 10 1993 aged 75
R.I.P.

A53

Kerb

In loving memory of **Eunice Carley**
who died 13th Dec. 1935 aged 83 years
Also of her beloved husband **George Carley**
who died 27th October 1952 aged 95 years
At rest

A54A

Brass plaque

Remembrance
Marjorie Grace Last
1921 – 1998

A55

Kerb

To the revered memory of a true Christian and loyal friend
Walter Seymour Knight
passed on towards the light September 11th 1935 aged 70 years

---

A56

Headstone
with kerb

In ever loving memory
of
Caroline Goldsmith
who died Janry 25th 1931
aged 72 years
Also of her beloved husband
Thomas Alfred Goldsmith
who died Febry. 5th 1939
aged 77 years
They bid farewell to no one
They said good-bye to none
The heavenly gates were opened
And a gentle voice said "Come"

A57

Kerb

In loving memory of **Edith Martha** wife of George Wenham
Born 15th Febry. 1869 died 1st Janry 1929
Also of **Rhoda Wenham** Born 11th November 1866
Died 12th April 1937

A58

Cross and kerb

In
loving memory
of
Esther
beloved wife of
James Burchett
Died 20th October 1922
aged 58 years
"For ever with the Lord"
Also of
Amy Ethel
daughter of
Esther and James Burchett
Died 3rd January 1895
aged 15 months

A59

Cross and kerb

In
loving memory
of
Harriot Hunnard
who died 17th February 1908
aged 80 years

A60

Cross and kerb

In loving memory
of
Henry Jones
who fell asleep
December 29th 1906 aged 76
Also of his wife
Emily Anne Jones
who fell asleep
on July 22nd 1923 aged 84
In death they were not divided
"At rest"

A61

Cross and kerb

In memory of
Gilbert Thomas
"Mannie"
infant son of T. and L. Mackness
of Wimbledon
Died 22nd May 1906 aged 17 months
At rest

A62

Headstone
and kerb

In
loving memory
of
George Saunders
who passed to his rest
24th January 1901
aged 60 years
"So He giveth His beloved sleep"
Also of
Catherine Saunders
who entered into rest
11th June 1929
aged 86 years
Beloved of their children and friends

A63

Headstone

In
loving memory
of
William Clift
who died December 6th 1892
aged 75 years
Also of **Emily Bourne**
beloved wife of the above
who died April 9th 1893
aged 67 years
We have to mourn the loss of two,
we did our best to save
Beloved on earth, regretted, gone
remembered in the grave

A64

Three tiered plinth
- top missing

In
loving memory
of
my dear wife
Annie Elizabeth Clay
who died 5th Nov. 1940
aged 58 years

A65

Cross and kerb

In
loving memory
of
Herbert Langford Wilson
Died March 14th 1937
aged 56 years
He was spared the pain of parting
He was spared all mortal strife
It was scarcely dying he only passed
in a moment to endless life

A66

Headstone
and kerb

In
loving memory
of
Louisa Thatcher
who died Sept. 7th 1934
aged 87 years
Go home my friends and shed no tears
In peace wait till Christ appears
Long was my time, long is my rest
God took me when He thought it best

A66P

Plaque

In loving memory of **Phoebe Turner**
who died Oct. 11th 1890
aged 24 years

A67

Headstone

In
loving memory
of
James Charles Guy
who died 15th Nov. 1918
aged 46 years
Also of
Annie wife of the above
who died on 4th February 1927
aged 53 years
"Thy will be done"

A68*

Headstone
and kerb

In loving memory
of
Ernest Edward
third son of
Walter and Caroline Hunt
born 20th May 1877
Died August 25th 1893
Watch and pray: for ye know
not when the time is   Mark XIII. 33
Also of their daughter
Caroline Alice Hunt
Died May 28th 1961
Also of **Emma** fourth daughter
and beloved wife of George Bennett
Died August 24th 1929 aged 44 years
Also of **Walter**, beloved husband of Caroline Hunt
died January 12th 1930 aged 81 years
Also of **Caroline Hunt** died June 14th 1936 aged 56 years   *"Reunited"*

★ Note - **Ernest Edward Hunt** died two days after being kicked by a horse; he was 16 years old

---

A68P*

Plaque

In memory of
Herbert S. Hemsley
who fell asleep in Jesus
22nd May 1895
aged 12 years
"Behold - I come quickly
Rev. III. 11

★ Note - **Herbert Hemsley** died of meningitis.

26

A69

Headstone

In
loving memory of
Frances Naomi
the beloved wife of James Guy
who died 10th Febry 1901
aged 28 years
Had He asked us well we know
we should cry and spare this blow
Yes with streaming tears should pray
Lord we love her let her stay"

———

A70

Headstone

In loving memory
of
Thomas Streeter
who died December 22nd 1906
aged 76 years
Lord I have loved the habitation of thy house
and the place where thine honour dwelleth
Psalms XXVI. 8
Also of **Mary**
the beloved wife of the above
who died April 3rd 1909
aged 75 years
My soul longeth for the courts of the Lord Psalms
LXXXIV. 2

———

A71*

Cross and kerb

In
loving memory
of
Daniel Alfred Ernest
son of
Frederick & Mary Allcorn
Died Octr. 19th 1907
aged 8 years
Jesus took a child and set him by Him
Luke IX. 47

* Note – **Daniel Alfred Ernest Allcorn**, known as **Ernest**, died of appendicitis

27

A72

Headstone
and kerb

In
loving memory
of **George Arnold**
second son of
George & Mary Rogers
who died August 17th 1908
aged 34 years
Lead, kindly light
Also of
George Rogers
who died May 7th 1929
aged 82 years

A73

Headstone
and kerb

In
loving memory
of
Annie Arms
who entered into rest 9th July 1923
aged 53 years
"Absent from the body, present with the Lord"

A73P

Flower Urn

In memory of
Lydia Hylands
29.4.24

A74

Rough hewn
granite cross and
base

In loving memory of
Cordelia Rickett
who passed away Jan. 13 1930
aged 68
"To me to live is Christ, And to die is gain"
May light eternal shine upon her O Lord"

A75A

Flower vase

Arthur Goldsmith
Louisa Goldsmith
Frank A. Roffey

A76

Headstone
and kerb

In loving memory of **Henry Marmaduke Langdale** beloved
husband of Rose Ellen Langdale
Died May 28th 1929 aged 80 years
And of **Rose Ellen Langdale** his dearly loved wife
Died September 10th 1931
aged 77 years
Blessed are the dead who die in the Lord
Henry Marmaduke Langdale
1929
Rose Ellen Langdale
1931

A77

Cross and kerb

In
loving memory
of
Vera Constance
eldest daughter of William
and Amelia Elizabeth Wisbey
of Westminster, London, S.W.1.
who died September 23rd 1925
aged 11 years 5 months
Jesus called a little child unto Him St. Matt. XVIII. 2
Peace, perfect peace
In
loving memory
of
Harriet Ann Wisbey
the beloved wife of
Willie Wisbey
of Halland
who died June 26th 1932
aged 72 years
And we know that all things work
together for good to them that
love God
Romans VIII. 28
In
loving memory
of
Willie Wisbey
of
Halland
who died August 8th 1937
aged 75 years
Be of good courage and He shall
strengthen your heart all ye that
hope in the Lord Psalm XXXI. 24
Reunited
Also of
William Wisbey
Died July 21st 1953 aged 63
They shall rest from their labours

A78

Headstone
and kerb

In
loving memory
of
Sarah Bennett
who died August 3rd 1918
aged 62 years
*"Father into thy hands I commend
my spirit"*
Also of **William**
the beloved husband of the above
who departed this life
January 4th 1932
"At rest"

A79*

Headstone
and kerb

In
loving memory
of
Fanny
the beloved wife of
Reginald George Walter
who died February 17 1910
aged 29 years
*Blessed are the pure in heart
for they shall see God Matt V.8*
Also of **Kitty**
the beloved second daughter of
John and Annie Burtenshaw
who died July 26th 1925
aged 19 months

★ Note – **Kitty Burtenshaw** was christened **Sarah Kate,** and I believe that Fanny Walter was her aunt on her mother's side of the family.

A80

Headstone
and kerb

In loving memory
of
Mary the beloved wife of
James Hall
who fell asleep December 29th 1906
aged 64 years
With Christ which is far better
Also of the above named
James Hall
who died June 16th 1917
aged 72 years
At rest

A81

Kerb and cross

In loving memory
of
my sister
Augusta Carr
Died October 25th 1916
Peace after pain
then a light
With God the rest

A82

Headstone and
footstone

In loving memory
of
Mary Ann
the beloved wife of
Edward Parris
of this parish
who departed this life Sept. 21 1903
aged 65 years
Thy will be done
Also of the above named
Edward Parris
who fell asleep April 5th 1908
aged 70 years
In God have I put my trust
I will not be afeared
(Footstone: M.A.P.   1903   E.P. 1908)

A83

Headstone

In
loving memory
of
Elizabeth
the beloved wife of
George Smith
who died March 30th 1907
aged 63 years
"Father, in thy gracious keeping,
leave we now thy servant sleeping"
Also of **George Smith**
who died March 8th 1909
aged 64 years

A84

Headstone
and kerb

In loving memory of
Samuel Novis
Died April 11th 1924
aged 74 years
Also
Lucy Novis
Died March 24th 1931
aged 77 years
At rest

A85

Headstone
and kerb

In
loving memory of
Kitty Cottingham
Died 15th April 1930
aged 83 years
Also of
William Cottingham
husband of the above
Died 20th Jany. 1931
aged 82 years
Absent from the body, present with the Lord

A86

Headstone
and kerb

In
loving memory
William Glue
"Gluie"
who died July 2nd 1946
aged 84 years
Great peace have they which love the Lord"

*A section of an old postcard showing the marker for Margaret Whapham,
No. A43*

SECTION B

SECTION B
B87 - 121

B87

Headstone

Until
the
day break
and the
shadows
flee away
In memory
of
my dear sister
Elizabeth Jane Stokes
who died 30th June 1924
"Thy will be done"

B88

Headstone
and kerb

In memory
of
Emily Heasman
Died February 8th 1937
aged 52
Also of her husband
Albert Edward Heasman
Died June 14th 1947
aged 74

B89

Headstone
and kerb

In loving memory
of
my beloved husband
David Cottingham
At rest June 22nd 1941
aged 63 years
"I will be to thee a shield"
Also of a devoted wife and mother
Ada Cottingham
Re-united September 26th 1961
Aged 79 years
Resting

B90

Red granite head-
stone and kerb

In loving memory of
Blanche Bennett
Died 20th May 1949
aged 53 years
Abide with me

B91

Headstone
and kerb

In loving memory of
a devoted husband and father
Henry Ashdown
who entered into rest 5th July 1939
aged 83 years
Also of his wife **Ellen**
a loving wife and mother
who fell asleep 14th August 1943
aged 87 years
Reunited
Rodney St. Vincent Stevens 1896 - 1968

B91PA

Plaque

Also
**Hilda May
Stevens**
Died 12th January 1979
Re-united

B92

Red granite cross
and rough hewn
plinth

In loving memory of
Margaret Fielding
daughter of
Peter & Mary Fielding
of Handforth, Cheshire
passed to her rest
22nd Nov. 1925
aged 81 years
For 20 years an ardent
worker together with God
for the good of this Parish

B93

Rough hewn cross
and plinth and
kerb

In
loving memory of
Anne E. Playne
Died Jan. 19th 1940
aged 85 years
Also of
Alfred Henry Playne
Died March 14th 1942
aged 90 years

B94

Granite cross on
rough hewn base
with kerb

In memory of
Alice Margaret Gould
September 3, 1921
Also in loving memory of
Harry Wyndham Gould
Died January 6th 1933 aged 55 years
Rest with Jesus

B94PA

Plaque

To the memory of **Millicent Gould**
Died Sept. 27th 1973
aged 84
second wife to Harry
God is love

B95

Headstone
and kerb

In loving memory
of
William Hellier
Born at Uffculme, Devon
August 18th 1832
Died April 21st 1918
Go thou faithful unto death and
I will give thee a crown of life

B95P

Plaque

In loving memory
of
William Turner
born 5th August 1831
Died 31st July 1914
Also of
Charlotte wife of the above
Born 12th April 1837
Died 16th March 1918

B96

Headstone
and kerb

In
loving memory
of
Margaret Booker
who passed away 19th December 1911
aged 51 years
*Blessed are the dead which die in the Lord
for they rest from their labours
Rev. XIV 13*

B96P

Plaque

In loving memory of
Alfred Guy
Postman for 33 years
Chiddingly & Whitesmith
Died 6th April 1908
aged 51

B97

Headstone

In loving memory
of
Mary Ann
wife of Alfred Elphick
who departed this life Jan. 4th 1902
aged 85 years
Also of the above named
Alfred Elphick
who departed this life Feb. 10th 1902
aged 88 years
They were lovely and pleasant in their lives
and in their death they were not divided
II Samuel 1. 23
They rest from their labours
Rev. XIV. 13

B98

Headstone

In loving memory
of
Isabel Violet Morley
who died June 27th 1904
aged 11 years
Not gone from memory nor from love
but gone to her Father's home above

B99

Headstone and
footstone

In loving memory
of
Eliza
wife of William Littlewood
Died April 9th 1899
aged 60 years
Also of the above named
William Littlewood
Died April 24th 1900
aged 63 years
Precious in the sight of the Lord is the
death of his saints
Psalm CXVI. 15
(Footstone – E.L. 1899   W.L. 1900)

40

B100

Headstone
and kerb

In
loving memory
of
Thomas Mullard
late Police Constable
of this Parish
who died 2nd October 1896
aged 49 years
God is our refuge and strength
a very present help in trouble
Also of **Mary Eliza**
the beloved daughter of
the above Thomas Mullard
and Mary his wife
who died 17th September 1896
aged 15 years
Blessed are the pure in heart
Also of **Mary** widow of the above
who died 20th March 1920
aged 72 years
interred at Bolton, Lancs.

B101

Kerb

Rest in Peace
In loving memory of **John Turner**
who died 6th April 1925 aged 65
Also of **Emma** his wife
who died 19th July 1938

B102*

Cross

In
loving memory
of
John Percy Turner
Died November 4th 1893
aged 4 years and 9 months
Not lost but gone before
R.I.P.

*Note – **John Percy Turner**, known as **Percy**, died as the result of a fall.

41

B103

Headstone

In loving memory
of
Frederick Turner
late of this Parish
Blacksmith
who died August 15th 1891
aged 65 years
Also of **Charlotte**
wife of the above
who died January 28th 1911
aged 80 years

B104*

Cross, plinth
and kerb

Sacred to the memory of
Alfred Durrant
Died Oct. 23rd 1893 aged 42 years
Until the day break
And of his wife
Elizabeth Annie
who died July 28th 1927
R.I.P.

* Note – **Elizabeth Annie Durrant-Grant** in Burials Register

B105

Open book

In memory of
our dear mother
Elsie L
Buckley
Died
9th September 1939
aged 51

and
our dear father
William W. Buckley
Died 30th Oct. 1963
aged 82

B106

Headstone

In
Loving memory of
**George Thwaites
Wright**
who died 17th Jan. 1940
aged 72 years
Also of his wife
Mary Jane
who died 8th Nov. 1940
aged 72 years

B107

Kerb

In loving memory of
our dear sister **Helen Hillier** died 27th September 1891
aged 24 years

B108

Kerb

In loving memory of
our dear son **Alfred Jack Guy** died July 21st 1940
aged 31 years

B109*

Headstone and
footstone

Erected by their family
In loving memory
of
Charles Booker
who died 6th September 1891
aged 58 years
Also **Ellen**, widow of the above
who died 4th October 1896
aged 56 years
Also **Charles** their son
who died in India 2nd August 1892
Footstone – C.B. 1891   E.B. 1896   C.B. 1892

*Note – The footstone to this grave has been moved next to the headstone and it now
obscures the quotation.

B110

Headstone

In
loving memory
of
John Webb
who died 31st Decr. 1940
aged 87 years
Also of
Elizabeth Ruth Webb
wife of the above
who died 6th August 1947
aged 73 years

B110P

Flower vase

**Rose Matilda
Richardson**
Died 1st Jan. 1941
Not forgotten

B111

Headstone

In loving memory
of
George Seymour
who died January 20th 1892
aged 61 years
"In the midst of life we are in death"
Also in loving memory of
Mary his wife
who passed away March 28th 1920
in her 87th year

B112

Headstone

In memory
of
Emily Mary
eldest daughter of the late
Frederick and Charlotte Turner
of this Parish
Passed onwards 15th June 1929
aged 76 years
A life that sacrificed much for others

B113

Open book

In
loving memory of
**Elizabeth Jane
Jeffery**
Died Sept. 11 1921
aged 40 years

Also of her husband
**Frederick
George**
died May 17th 1943
aged 63 years
Re-united

B114

Headstone

In
loving memory
of
Percival William
the beloved youngest son of
Herbert and Harriett Funnell
who passed peacefully away
9th June 1918
aged 26 years
Gone from us, but not forgotten
Never shall his memory fade;
sweetest thoughts shall ever linger
around this spot where he is laid"
Also of his brother
Herbert Charles Funnell
who died 30th July 1949
aged 62 years

B115

Headstone

In
loving memory
of
our dear mother and father
Elizabeth Moore
who died August 18th 1939
Timothy Moore
who died August 22nd 1923
aged 69

45

B116

Kerb

In loving memory of
Amos the beloved husband of Rosetta Funnell
who died 9th December 1923 aged 58 years
Also **Rosetta Funnell** died September 20th 1938 aged 73 years
At Rest

B117

Kerb

Annie Cohn died 15th August 1929 aged 63
Harold Charles Cohn died 25th December 1932 aged 70

B118

Kerb

In loving memory of **Lucy Stepney**
died July 15th 1929 aged 77
Also of **Richard Stepney** died November 30th 1937 aged 88
At rest

B119*

Headstone

Mother
Sadly missed
Jan. 17 1933 aged 70
One of the dearest
one of the best
God in his mercy
called her to rest
A secret thought
a silent tear
keeps her memory
ever near
We miss her words
her kindly way
with her we spent
many happy days
We miss her when we
need a friend
on her we always
could depend
R.I.P.

*Note – This headstone is lying in the middle of the grave for Lucy Stepney. On consulting the Burial Register the only entry which fits the date is for **Sarah Jane Cosham**, who was buried on the 21st January 1933.

B120

Black polished
granite cross on
plinth

In loving memory of
John Clarke
who entered into rest
March 19th 1930
aged 57
Also the wife of the above
Rose Emily Clarke
Died March 6th 1966
aged 97

B121

Kerb

In loving memory of our dear parents
Richard H. Copp passed away 20th Sept. 1949 aged 83
Helen Copp passed away 21st Jany 1950 aged 84

East Hoathly War Memorial

48

SECTION C

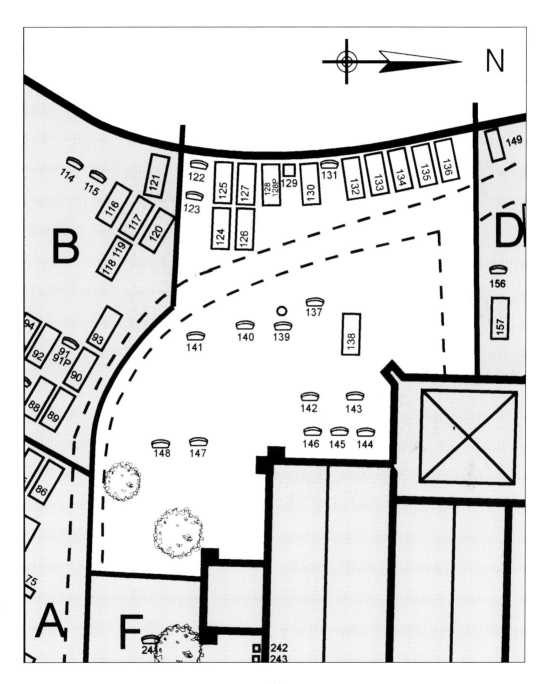

N

C122

Headstone

In loving memory
of
Frank Wright
who departed this life
13th August 1939 aged 74 years
"The day thou gavest, Lord, is ended
Also **Caroline**
his beloved wife
who passed peacefully away
26th April 1953 aged 85 years

───────────

C123

Headstone

In grateful remembrance of
Ellen Billenness
Died February 4th 1942
aged 71 years
and of
Ebenezer Billenness
Died September 20th 1953
aged 81 years
Loved parents and grandparents
Resting Rev. 14.13
Waiting Rom. 8.23

───────────

C124

Headstone
and kerb

In
loving memory of
Ada Clara
the beloved wife of
William Heasman
who passed peacefully away
27th June 1939 aged 78 years
"To await the coming of the Lord"
Also **William Heasman** her husband
who passed peacefully away
March 28th 1943 aged 85 years
"And they rest from their labours"

C125

Kerb

In loving memory of
my dear wife **Alice Kate
Turner** who died 22nd Feb. 1938 aged 49 years
In God's keeping

C126

Kerb

Frederick Thomas Westgate
who died 22nd May 1937 aged 53 years
Also his wife **Alice Westgate**
died 27th August 1949 aged 65 years
Re-united

C127

Headstone
and kerb

In loving memory
of
John Burton
Died Jan. 8th 1937 aged 73 years
Also
Ruth Burton
sister of the above
Died Jan. 11th 1949 aged 78 year

C128

Kerb and
open book

In loving
memory of
my dear husband
**Sampson B.
Thorpe**
Died 22nd Sept. 1935
aged 72
years

Also of
**Emma
Thorpe**
his beloved wife
Died 11th March 1940
aged 75
years
At rest

C128PA

Plaque

Daisy May Thorpe
Perfect Peace
Died Nov. 22nd 1959
aged 66

C129

Stone inset
in ground

In
memory of
Kathleen Bishop
beloved mother
1904-1935

C130

Kerb

In loving memory of a beloved husband and father
Alfred Henry Ellis who died 19th May 1935 aged 70
Also of **Annie Maria** his beloved wife
who died 20th April 1946 aged 77 years

C131*

Headstone

In
memory of
Kate Lester
Died 5th May 1935
aged 62
"At rest"

*Note – Registered as **Eliza Kate Lester** in Burials Register

---

C132*

Two tiered cross
and kerb

In loving memory
of
**Dorothea
Lilian**
dearly loved wife of
Fred Andrew Cull
who died Dec. 11th 1934 aged 35
"Till we meet again"
In loving memory of our dear daughter **Dorothea Lilian Cull**
Died Dec. 11th 1934 aged 35
Also of **Annie Westgate** Died April 9th 1959 aged 72 years

* Note - **Dorothea Lilian Cull** was a Westgate before her marriage, and **Annie Westgate** was an aunt.

52

C133

Headstone
and kerb

In
loving memory
of
my beloved wife
Mercy Gurr
who died 13th October 1934
aged 73 years
"He hath done all things well"
Also of **John Gurr**
husband of the above
who died 29th April 1950
aged 76 years
"He's gone in endless bliss to dwell"

C134

Kerb

In loving memory of
our dear parents **George & Ann Pankhurst**

C135

Kerb

In loving memory of **Harry Barden**
Died 31st July 1932 aged 58 years
In loving memory of **Hannah** his wife
Died 12.4.56 aged 79

C136

Headstone
and kerb

In loving memory of
George Henry Burton
of Halland
Died 18th April 1932 aged 71
"At rest"
Also of **Sarah Ann**
his wife
Died 25th March 1941
aged 83 years

C137

Headstone

Sacred
to the memory of
John Pankhurst
who departed this life
July 26th 1875
aged 31 years
"In the midst of life we are in death
How sweet to sleep in Jesus!"

C138

Rough hewn
granite block
and kerb

In
loving memory
of
Albert Edward Turner
Passed away
27th September 1930
aged 61 years
At rest
Also of his wife
Clara Shaw Turner
passed away 15th May 1949

C139

Headstone

To the memory
of
Thomas Rich
an old and respected inhabitant
of this Parish
who died the 11th day of Novr. 1877
aged 80 years
His end was peace
Also of **Jane** the beloved wife
of the above
who died Feb. 15th 1887
in the 88th year of her life
Thy will be done

C139*

Iron marker

George Leeson
Jan. 25th 1885
83 years

★ Note – This is an iron marker leaning on the headstone for **Thomas Rich**. It does not indicate the burial place of **George Leeson**

C140

Headstone

Sacred
to the memory of
Martha
wife of John Turner
of this Parish
who died Sept. 15th 1868
aged 63 years
Also of
John Turner
who died May 25th 1888
aged 88 years

C141

Headstone

In
loving memory
of
Ann
the beloved wife of
William Evenden
who fell asleep August 30th 1916
Aged 74 years
Also of
Winifred Annie
younger daughter of above named
who fell asleep November 13th 1871
aged 5 years
Resting
Also the above named
William Evenden
who fell asleep October 28th 1921
aged 84 years
At Rest

C142

Headstone

Henry Rich
Born 30th April 1886
Died 27th September 1947

C143*

Headstone

In memory
of
Henry Rich
who died August 19th 1867
aged 81 years
For 57 years
he faithfully performed the duties
of this Parish
of which he was a resident
throughout his life
Also in memory of
Sarah his widow
who died May 19th 1870
aged 83

* Note – Henry Rich had been Parish Clerk for 57 years

C144

Headstone

To the memory of
Sarah Coates
who departed this life
July 28th 1855
aged 54 years

C145

Double sided
headstone

In memory of
Frances Rich
the wife of
Henry Rich, Junr.
who died Jany 9th 1855
aged 43 years
Also of
the above named
Henry Rich Junr.
who died Octr. 11th 1863
aged 52 years

Also in memory of
Three children of
Henry & Frances Rich
viz.
Elizabeth Died Feb. 23: 1836
Aged 10 weeks
George Died April 10: 1839
aged 10 weeks
Sarah Jane Died Dec. 20: 1847
aged 14 months

C146

In memory of
Mary Ann
wife of Albert Henry Rich
who died March 23rd 1875
aged 30 years
Why do we mourn departed friends
or shake at deaths alarms
Tis but the voice that Jesus sends
to call them to His arms

C147

In
loving memory
of **Edith Mary**
second daughter of
Alfred and Mary Trill
of this Parish
who died 8th September 1875
aged 2 years and 6 months
Also of
Herbert their youngest son
who died 10th December 1908
aged 25 years
"Jesu, lover of my soul"

C148

In
ever loving memory
of
Alfred Trill
who passed peacefully away
2nd February 1918
aged 83 years
"Until the day break"
Also of
Mary his beloved wife
who was called home
11th December 1925
aged 86 years
"Light at evening time"

58

SECTION D

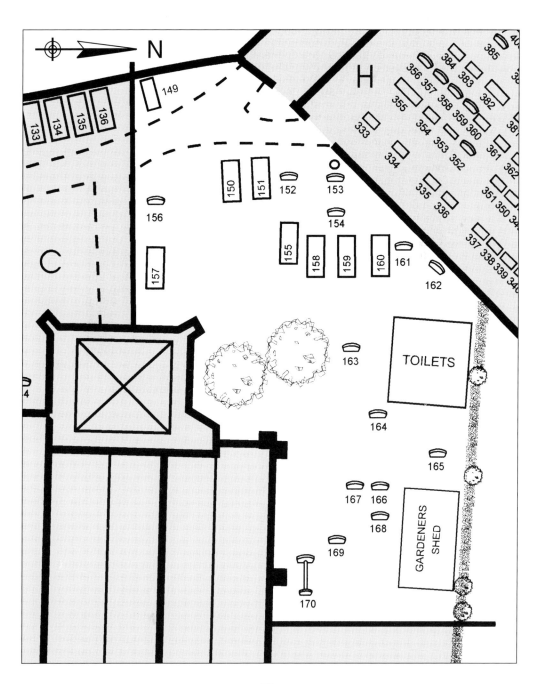

SECTION D
D149 – 170

D149

Kerb

In loving memory of our dear little son
Michael Robin Helsdon
whom God called to Himself 15th August 1934 aged 7 weeks

⊷══────────────══⊷

D150

Kerb

In loving memory of **Mary Barber**
who died March 15th 1923 aged 86 years
Peace perfect peace

⊷══────────────══⊷

D151

Headstone

In loving memory
of
George Burton
of Halland
who died March 15th 1914
aged 78 years
"I shall be satisfied when I awake
with Thy likeness Psa. 17. 15
Also of **Sarah**
his beloved wife
who fell asleep Nov. 1st 1919
aged 79 years
He will fulfil the desire of them
that fear him Psa. 145. 19
"Forever with the Lord"

D152

Headstone

In
loving memory of
George   Bennett
who died March 27th 1909
aged 75 years
*The Lord gave and the Lord hath taken
away; blessed be the name of the Lord Job 1. 21*
Also of **Harriet**
wife of the above
who died April 7th 1919 aged 75 years
Thy will be done

D153

Headstone

In
loving memory
of
our dear father & mother
John Carey
Died 12th December 1907
aged 78 years
Eliza Carey
Died 24th October 1915
aged 82 years
*"Nothing in my hand I bring
Simply to the cross I cling*

D153*

Iron marker

George Carey
20th April 1888
22 years

★ Note – This is one of the iron markers mentioned in the Introduction. It is leaning
against the gravestone for John Carey and does not indicate the place of burial.

D154

Headstone

In
loving memory
of
Henry Norman
of East Hoathly
who died August 12th 1899
aged 71 years
"He hath done all things well"
Mark VIII. 37
Also of **Hannah**
beloved wife of the above
who died December 17th 1905
aged 81 years

D155

Headstone
and kerb

In
loving memory
of
Alexander Brakefield
who was taken to his rest
14th March 1906
aged 62 years
Thou wilt keep him in perfect peace
Also of **Mary**
wife of the above
who fell asleep 15th Dec. 1923
aged 84 years
Calm and sweet repose

D156

Headstone

In loving memory
of
Samuel Starnes
who died 22nd January 1925
Also of
Jane Starnes
the beloved wife of the above
who died 30th March 1914
Asleep in Jesus

D157

Kerb

In loving memory of **Gladys Rosaline Hylands**
Died 19th May 1949 aged 29 years
Abide with me

D158

Kerb

In loving memory of **John Hampton**
Died May 9th 1937 aged 89 years
Also his wife **Laura** June 22nd 1937 aged 85
A devoted couple who lived and died together

D159

Headstone
and kerb

In loving remembrance
of
Sally
the beloved wife of
James Hampton
who entered into rest June 1st 1889
aged 73 years
*Come unto me, all ye that labour and are heavy
laden, and I will give you rest*
Also of the above named
James Hampton
(of Old Possingworth, Waldron, Sussex)
who entered into rest Nov. 23rd 1900
aged 76 years
*Mark the perfect man, and behold the upright
for the end of that man is peace*

D160

Polished pink
granite headstone
and rough hewn
kerb

In loving memory
of
my dear sister
Fanny
younger daughter of the late
James and Sally Hampton
Old Possingworth, Waldron
who entered into rest
14th May 1925
aged 66 years
He hath done all things well
Also of **Lois Hampton**
Died September 6th 1938
aged 81 years
Thy will be done

D161

Headstone

In loving memory
of
Thomas Funnell
late of Laughton
Born December 15th 1823
Died January 10th 1890
There the wicked cease from troubling;
and there the weary be at rest
Job 3. 17

D162

Plaque

In loving [memory]
of
Martha Tu[rner]
who died March [1899]
aged 51 years
Also of her husband
Robert Turner
who died June 24th 1934
aged 86 years

D163

Headstone

In memory of
Mary daughter of William
and Ann Bye
late of Suffolk
who died Nov. [21st] 1805
aged 20 years
While in this world I did remain
My days wear [   ] with grief & pain
At length the Lord did think it best
To take me to my place of rest

D164

Headstone

Sacred
to the memory of
Jeremiah
affectionate son of James
and Sally Hampton
who died Octr. 25th 1874
in his 20th year
God is love

D165

Headstone

Sacred
to the memory
of **Walter Fuller Tilly**
who departed this life
4th of February
1862
aged 50 years
Also of
Hannah widow of the above
who died at Eastbourne
30th May 1886
aged 80 years
*"There remaineth therefore a
rest to the people of God"* Hebrews IV. 9

D166

Headstone

Sacred
to the memory of
Henry
son of
James & Sally Hampton
who died 11th April 1854
aged 3 years
We cannot tell who next may fall
beneath his chastising rod
one must be first, but let us all
prepare to meet our God

D167

Headstone

In memory of
William Hampton
who died 16th September
MDCCCLIII
aged 73 years
Also of **Frances** his wife
who died 7th February 1846
aged 58 years
and of **Phoebe** their daugh
ter (wife of William Witbourn)
who died 7th October 1840
aged 22 years

D168

Headstone

In memory of
Hammont Engledow
who departed this life March 1st 1826
aged 82 years
Also of
Mrs. [Sarah] Engledow
First wife of the above
who departed this life
April 15th 1802 aged 73
Also of **Maria Culpeck**
niece of the above
Mr. Hammont Engledow
who departed this life
Dec. 12th 1825 aged 28 years

D169

Headstone

Thy will be done
In loving remembrance
of
Emily
wife of George Douglas Berry
who died September 20th 1891
aged 30 years
In the midst of live we are in death
Also of **George Douglas**
son of the above
who died June 16th 1891
aged 14 months
Suffer little children to come unto me

D170

Headstone and
footstone with
connecting board

In sacred memory of
Mrs. Susan Walls
late of this Parish
who died June 11th 1808
aged 83 years
Also of **Mr. Thomas Walls**
husband of the above
who died April 22nd 1815
aged 84 years
And of **Ann Vine** their
granddaughter
who died Sept. 13th 1799
aged 6 months

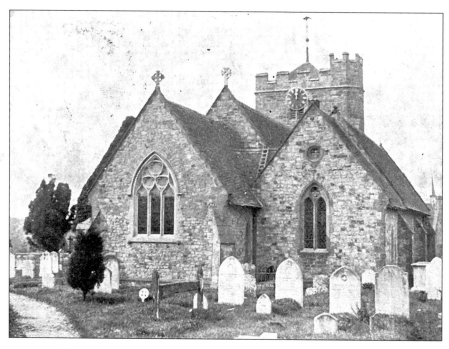

Postcard of East Hoathly church showing the 'bedboard' grave marker and a white painted cast iron marker

SECTION E

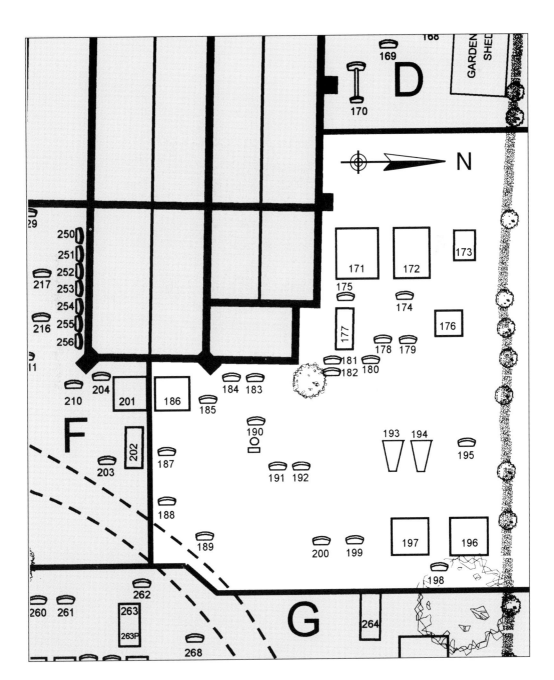

69

SECTION E
A1 – 86

E171

Tomb

Sacred
to the memory of
Mary daughter of
Henry & Mary Holman
who died 1st May 1840 aged 6 years
Also of **Susanna Martin**
their daughter
who died 1st January 1848
aged 18 years
And of
Jane Colgate
daughter of the above
Henry & Mary Holman
who died
at Pau-Basses, Pyrenees
16th May 1856
aged 28 years
The blood of Jesus Christ his son cleanseth us from all sin

E172

Cross and kerb

In memory of
Henry Holman
who practised as surgeon
in this parish
for upwards of 65 years
Born June 24th 1802 died Decr. 5th 1890
"Whoso trusteth in the Lord, happy is he Prov. XVI 16. 20
Also of
Mary his wife
born March 28th 1800
died May 20th 1893
*Her children arise up and call
her blessed
Prov XXXI. 28*

E173

Tiers.
Cross broken off

Francis Edward
Born Decr. 8th 1861
Died Septr. 5th 1862
William
born February 14th 1863
Died July 27th 1863
Wilfred Eastment
born Novr. 2nd 1868 died Feb. 2nd 1870
the beloved children of
Henry Colgate and Jane Meade Holman

———

E174

Headstone

To the memory
of
Mercy, Relict
of Arthur Brook
late of Wilmington
in this county
who died 25th Nov. 1764
aged 78 years

———

E175

Headstone

In memory
of **Mrs. Eliz. Hicks**
who died March 30th 1771
aged 79 years

———

E176*

Plinth with
draped urn

In memory of
Janet wife of
Alexander Snodgrass
Born in Renfrewshire
1813
Died in this parish
31st August 1882

* Note – On the 14th April 1916 the local paper reported the funeral of the late Mr. A. Snodgrass. He was interred in a grave beside that of his mother, Janet, who had died at Whyly on 31st August 1882. There is no headstone marking his grave.

E177

Chest

Sacred to the memory of
Mr. Philip Turner
late of this Parish, Mercer, who
departed this life
[ ] December 1829
aged 60 years
Sacred to the memory of
Mrs. Sarah Turner wife of
Mr. Philip Turner of this parish
Mercer who died April 10th 1814
aged 36 years
Also of **Stephen Martin Turner** their son
who died the same day aged 13 days
And of **Audrey Batley Turner** their
daughter Obt April 7th 1825
aged 16 years
Mr.
Michael Turner
late of this parish
Mercer
died July 8th 1810
aged 37 years
Susanna Martin
daughter of Philip
& Sarah Turner
died January 5th 1827
aged 25 years
Charlotte Martin daughter
of Philip and Sarah Turner died 4th July
1828 aged 23 years
Sarah Martin their daughter
died 15th Nov. 1828 aged 25 years

E178

Headstone

In
memory of **Thomas Turner** of
this Parish Draper who died
February 6th 1793 aged 63 years
And of **Margaret** daughter
of the said Thomas Turner
by Mary his wife who departed
this life August 28th 1791
aged 25 years

E179

Headstone

To the memory of **Peter** son of
Thomas and Mary Turner of
this parish who died July 1st
1786 aged 18 years
The Lord hath brought down my strength
in my journey and shortened my day but
His mercy is from everlasting to everlasting
upon them that fear Him
Also of **Frederick** son of the
said Thomas and Mary Turner
who died an infant

E180

Headstone

In memory of
Theodosia
wife of
William Johnson
Born 3rd January 1818
died 26th July 1886
"Them also which sleep in Jesus
will God bring with Him I Thes. IV. 14
Also of the above named
William Johnson
late of Waldron Sussex
born 21st July 1798
died 22nd September 1891

E181

Headstone

In loving memory
of
Jane Ealing
who fell asleep in Jesus
October 26th 1888
aged 75 years
Her end was peace

E182

Headstone

In loving memory of **Sally Clark**
who fell asleep in Jesus January 20th 1882 aged 61 years
Her end was peace

E183

Headstone

In memory
of **William Cayley**
who departed this
life ye 25th of February
1751 aged
53 years

E184

Headstone

In
memory of
Susanna the wife
of William Cayley
late of this Parish
who departed this
life the 9th of
December 1771
aged 74 years

E185

Cross

Mary Ann
wife of [Charles] Kemp
[ ] 1874 [39] years

E186

Polished black
granite slab and
kerb

Alfred Davidson Allan
of Singapore
and of Fir Grove in this Parish
Born Adelaide, South Australia
Died April 8th 1938 at Fir Grove
Aged 69
and
Frances Margaret
wife of the above
born Melbourne, Australia
died April 8th 1961 at Eastbourne
aged 80
"Reunited"
A.D.A.

E187

Headstone

In
loving memory of
**Christopher Ridley
Richardson**
1893 - 1965
Pilot and Chaplain R.A.F.
Rector of this Parish
1947 - 1961
And of **Gwyneth Mary**
his wife
1896 - 1988
Conductor of many choirs

E188

Headstone

In the midst of life we are in death
Henry & Alfred Russell
who were accidentally drowned
at Eastbourne
June 11th 1876
aged respectively 21 and 18 years

E189

Headstone

In loving memory
of
Minnie Jane
elder daughter of Caleb
and Mary Jane Woodhams
who died August 22nd 1882
aged 2 years & 7 months
*"Suffer little children to come
unto me for of such is the Kingdom
of Heaven"*
Also of **Lilian Maud**
second daughter of the above
who died December 16th 1882
aged 4 months

E190

Headstone and
footstone

Here lieth the body of
John Spooner who de
parted this life March
27th 1730 aged 35 years
Kind reader stay and shed a tear
And shew the dust that lieth here
his glass is run, his breath is spent
his days are gone, his life was lent
(Footstone: J.S. 1730)

E190

Iron marker

Kate Page
19th June 1889
16 years

★ Note – This iron marker is resting against the gravestone for **John Spooner**. It does not
indicate the place of burial for **Kate Page**

E191

Headstone

In loving memory of
Louisa Patience Walker
taken whilst asleep
9th May 1886
aged 52 years
The dear wife
and faithful companion of
William Charles Walker
"For so He [   ]
Also of
Horace Radcliffe
son of the Rev. C. A. Walker
taken by Jesus May 16th 1890
aged 6 months
Such is the Kingdom of Heaven

E192

Headstone

In loving memory of
Henry James Sims
who fell asleep
8th April 1886
aged 29 years
Present with the Lord II Cor. V. 8

E193

Body stone

In memory of
Joseph Fuller Senr
late of this Parish
who died 6th March 1773
aged 75 years

E194

Body stone

To the memory of
Margaret wife of
[John] Fuller of Lewes
who died Sept. 25th 1753
aged 35 years

E195

Headstone

In memory
of **Willm**. **Fuller** who died
April 5th 1751 aged [4] years
Also
of **Ann Fuller** who died
April 24th 1751 aged 9 mon
Son & Daughtr of
Joseph and Mary Fuller

E196

Headstone
and kerb

In loving memory
of **George William Carey**
Eldest son
of
Peter and Loanna Ranger
who died at East Hoathly February 19th 1885
aged 18 years
"The Lord gave and the Lord hath taken away
Blessed be the name of the Lord"
Also of **Loanna Mary**
the beloved wife of Peter Ranger
who entered into rest June 14th 1919
aged 81 years
"So He giveth his beloved sleep"
Also of **Peter Ranger**
who died March 11th 1921
aged 78 years
"Peace perfect peace"

E197

Headstone
and kerb

In
loving memory
of
Isabel May
Eldest daughter of the late
John Carey Saunders
of Norfolk
who fell asleep in this Parish
31st December 1892
aged 14 years
Safe in the arms of Jesus

E198*

Headstone

Sacred
to the memory of
Samuel Carley
who died in Framfield
on the 15th March 1862
aged 61 years
Also of **Sarah** his widow
who died 22nd Octbr. 1864
aged 58 years

★ Note - **Sarah Carley** is entered in the Burials Register as **Sarah Garratt.** She married George Garratt, widower in Framfield on 20th July 1863.

E199

Headstone

Sacred
to the memory
of
Mary Rich
late of this Parish
who died 12th September
MDCCCXLIV
aged 54 years
This stone is erected in gratitude
to a kind parent by her daughter
Mary Russell

E200

Headstone

Elizabeth Rich
widow
who died 5th April 1885
aged 92 years
*"As in Adam all die even so in
Christ shall all be made alive"*

An example of Jonathan Harmer's terracotta panels

SECTION F

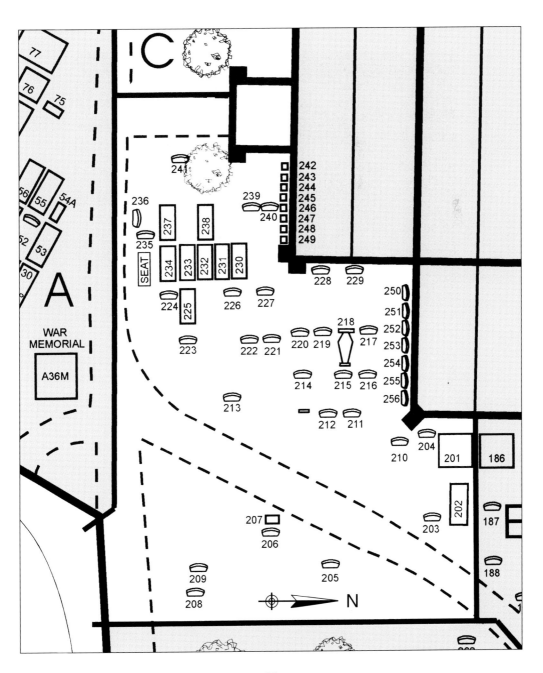

SECTION F
F201 – 256

F201*

Headstone
and kerb

In loving memory of
John Frederick Groves, M.A.
Rector of this Parish 1922 – 1933
who died 7th April 1933 aged 72 years
Behold the lamb of God which taketh away the sin of the world
John 1.29
Also of **Ethel Amelia Groves**
Died 22nd December 1934 aged 69 years

* Note – The Parish Registers state that the ashes of Sheila Flora Groves, who died aged 80 in South Africa, are buried in the family grave. It is noted that the ashes of Henry Basil Melvin Groves are also buried here, but there is no registration of this.

F202

William Hardy Johnson
Priest
1882-1947
R.I.P.

F203

Headstone with
hourglass

Here lieth the body
of **Richrd Chatfield**
who died ye 4th of

Octob^r 1730 aged
58 years

F204

Headstone with
Harmer panel

In memory of
Elizabeth daughr of John
and Sarah Wickerson
of this Parish, Spinster, who died
June 18th 1811 aged **29 years**
Reader stand and shed a tear
and view the dust that lieth here
Remember to repent in time
[she] was taken in her prime
Also of **Mary** their daughter
also Spinster who died June
5th 1813 aged 27 years
When Christ who is our life shall
appear then shall ye also appear
with Him in glory   Col. 3. Ver. 4

F205

Headstone

In affectionate remembrance
of
Kate Wain
Late of Brockhampton
Gloucestershire
who died at East Hothly
May 16th 1881
in the 21st year of her age
Sleep on thou blest one, sleep in peace
Thy pain and sorrow now doth cease
The narrow stream of death is crossed
and we are left to mourn thy loss

F206

Headstone, split

In memory of
Thomas Fuller
Tallow chandler
late of this Pa
rish
who died
the 20th of Fe
bruary 1762
aged 59 years

This stone erected
by his youngest son
James Fuller

F207

Plaque

In loving memory
of
William Warren
who died Aug. 12 1886
aged 18 years

F208

Headstone

In affectionate memory
of
Fanny Maria
the beloved wife of Mark Bristow
who died January 3rd 1882
aged 33 years
*She died with a good hope of a
resurrection*
Also of
Jane his second wife
who died August 12th 1897
aged 59 years

F209

Headstone

In
memory of
Matthew Colman
who died April 23rd 1883
aged 75 years
This stone is erected in recognition
of a long and faithful service

F210

Headstone

In loving memory
of
Walter Wickerson
who died 6th December 1893
aged 75 years
Also of **Susan** his wife
who died 21st March 1884
aged 65 years
Also of
Caroline Morton
who died 11th July 1886
aged 25 years
buried in Stoke Churchyard

F211

Headstone carved
with 3 angels and
2 trumpets

Rebekah Weller Died
Feb. 17 1728 aged 2 years
Ann Weller died Sep
6th 1729 aged 7 years
Mary Weller Died Mar[h]
6th 1732 aged 5 years
daughter of Francis
and Rebekah Weller

F212

Headstone

In loving remembrance
of
Hannah
the beloved wife of
David Hall
who departed this life Nov. 30th 1880
aged 74 years
Looking for that blessed hope, and the glorious
appearing of the great God and our Saviour
Jesus Christ. Titus 2.13
Also of
David Hall
who departed this life Nov. 12th 1888
aged 85 years
Thou which hast showed me great and sore troubles
Shalt quicken me again and shalt bring me up again
From the depths of the earth Psalms 71.20

F213*

Broken headstone
and very worn

[**Emy** daughter of John and Elizabeth Lovell
died August 1798 aged 8]
Also of **Elizabeth**
wife of John Lovell
Heathfield who died [September]1797
[aged 32]
Likewise of **John**
their son who died [July 1797 aged 1 month]

★ Note – This headstone is very worn and the top has been broken off. In a good light it
is possible to read some of it and the rest (in the square brackets) is guess work based on
information in the Parish Burial Register. There are only 3 Lovells buried in East
Hoathly Churchyard, and I think it is quite possible that they are all buried here.

F214

Headstone and
footstone

In memory
of
Joseph Burgess
of this Parish
Died March 8th 1780
Aged [62] years
Also of **Sarah** wife of
Joseph Burgess
Died [ ] July 1779

F215

Headstone

In memory of
Charles Russell
Died December 30th 1885
aged 68 years
Also of
Mary Noakes Russell
Wife of the above
Died November 23rd 1891
aged 72 years

F216

Headstone

In
memory of
Francis Weller
Mercer late of this Parish
who died Decembr 23rd 1748
aged 62 years
Also
of **Rebecca** his wife
who died July 21st 1763
aged 69 years

F217

Headstone

Sacred
to the memory of
Frances Burgess
who departed this life
the 19th of April
MDCCCLV
aged 49 years
Erected
To perpetuate the remembrance of
a kind daughter by her surviving parent
Jane Russell

F218

Body stone

In memory of
William Charles Bayley
son of John and Jane Bayley
(of Tenterden, Kent)
who departed this life
September 5th 1849
aged 3 years
and 5 months
Also of **Sarah Ann** their
daughter who died October [11th] 1849
aged 1 year and 10 months

F219

Headstone

In the memory of
Arthur Russell
son of
Charles & Jane Russell
who departed this life on
the 1st day of November 1840
aged 50 years

F220

Headstone

Sacred to the memory of
Charles Russell
who departed this life
the 24th June 1858
aged 72 years
Also of **Jane** his wife
who died 25th Decr. 1857
aged 78 years

F221*

Split headstone

To the memory of

Sarah Relict
of Josh Burges
late of this Parish
who died May 1763
aged 80 years

Also of **Mary**
wife of Tho. Davy
(and daughter of
the above Jos. & Sarah Burgis)
who died 30 Jan. 1775
aged 52 years

* Note – This is a divided headstone, the left hand side is carved with an urn and the right hand side with a crown and trumpets.

F222

Headstone with
central trumpets
with crown above
and leaves on
either side

In memory of
Thomas Davy
late of this Parish
who died August 27th 1801
aged 72 years
Also of **Wm**. and **Mary Gasson**
son & Daughter-in-law
of the above Thomas Davy
whose remains are inter'd
near this place

F223*

Headstone

Here lies
the body of
Richard Marchant
who died May [19th] 1757
Also of [**Mary** buried Feb 1 1766]

* Note - A very thick and well worn headstone. On the back is carved No. 1.
The information in the square brackets has been taken from the Parish Burial Register

F224

Headstone

In loving memory
Herbert Edward Hall
who departed this life Oct 1st 1879
aged 16 months
*Suffer little children come unto me
for of such is the kingdom of God
Luke XVIII. 16*
Also of
Albert Charles Hall
who departed this life April 17th 1880
aged 17 years
*Blessed are the dead which die in the Lord
Rev. XIV. 13*

F225

Kerb and plain
cross

In loving memory of **Fanny Georgina Hall**
who entered into rest
13th December 1916 aged 44 years

F226

Cross on plinth

In loving memory of
Hannah
the dearly beloved wife of
Richard Hall
who fell asleep 28th March 1915
aged 76 years
Peace perfect peace
Also of
Richard Hall
who entered into rest 31st Oct. 1934
aged 93 years
But now they desire a better country that is an heavenly
Hebrews XI. 16.

—⁃⊨⊙———————⊙⊨⁃—

F227

Headstone

In memory of
John Larking
who died 25th January
MDCCCLV
aged 54 years
Also of
Mercy Larking
the wife of Jn. Larking
who died 12th February
MDCCCLV
aged 54 years

—⁃⊨⊙———————⊙⊨⁃—

F228*

Ledger

Here lies the body
of the Reverend
Mr. Haworth late
Rector of this Parish
who departed this
life October $^{y}_{e}$ 25th

in $^{y}_{e}$ 61 year of

his age Anno

Domini 1718

* Note – This ledger is leaning against the church wall. It was removed from the bell
tower during renovation work.

F229

Headstone

Edward Raynes
of Belmont in this Parish
Died August 6th MDCCCXXXVIII
aged Liii years

———————

F230

Kerb

In loving memory of
beloved husband and father **John William Green**
who Died May 25th 1942 in his 59th year
Also of **Rosa Ann** his wife who died August 28th 1972 aged 89

———————

F230P

Plaque

In loving
memory of
Jack Green
who died
13th Sept. 1996
aged 82

———————

F231

Headstone and
kerb

In
affectionate remembrance
of
Emily Mary Jenner
Died 23rd July 1942
aged 83

———————

F232

Kerb

In loving memory of **Mary Martha Hurd**
died 17th September 1942 aged 75 years
Also of **Albert Ernest Hurd**
died Dec. 26th 1946 aged 80 years
Resting

———————

F233

Kerb

In loving memory of my dear husband
Arthur Frederick Finch passed on Nov. 19th 1942 aged 51

F234

Headstone
and kerb

In
loving memory
of
Fanny
beloved wife of
Walter Luther Kemp
Died January 22nd 1943
aged 77 years
Still to the mourner's heart he
comfort speaketh,
Fear not, believe, she is not dead
but sleepeth

F235

Headstone

Sacred
to the memory of
Charlotte the beloved wife of
Robert Burgess
who departed this life
Jan. 19th 1863
aged 62 years
Also of
Robert Burgess
who departed this life
July 21st 1863
aged 62 years
An affectionate and beloved
mother and father
For to me to live is Christ, and to die is gain
Philippians I. 21

F236A

Inset stone

Rosamund McIntosh
3rd October 1957
aged 13 years

F237

Kerb

In loving memory of
my beloved wife **Mildred Judd**
who died 25th July 1943 aged 81 years
Also of her husband **Samuel C. Judd**
who died 11th April 1952 aged 68 years
At Rest

F238

Kerb

In loving memory of
Frederick Corbett Hickie
Lt. Col. Indian Army
8th May 1888 – 28th July 1965
R.I.P.
In loving memory of
Mary Edith Rushton who died 28th April 1943 aged 70 years

F239

Headstone

Affectionate remembrance
of
David Paine
who died 30th May 1856
aged 66 years
Also of
Susanna his wife
who died 2nd March 1870
aged 83 years

F240*

Harmer plaque

In memory of
John Burgess
late of this Parish Victualler
who died June 18th 1810
aged 75 years
And of **Charity** his wife
who died Novr. 8th 1810
aged 69 years

*Note – This gravestone to John Burgess has an inset Harmer panel. See Introduction.

F241

Headstone

**Christiana Alice
Hunt**
Died May 14th 1945
aged 58 years
Also
**Robert James
Hunt**
Died Feb. 5th 1975
aged 85 years

F242A

In loving memory of
**Harry William
Hitchcock**
Born February 21st 1910
Died December 31st 1968
And my wife
**Marjorie Lena
Hitchcock**
Born August 25th 1904
Died February 15th 1974

F243A

Open book

In loving memory of
my dear mother
Edith Emma Winn
Died 10th Feb. 1961
in her 87th year
The Lord is my shepherd
Virtue et Labore

F244A

Slab

In fond memory
of
Henry W. J. Winn
Capt. R.A.
Died Feb. 21st 1964
aged 66
Virtue et Labore

F245A

Open book

In loving
memory of
my dear husband **F. C. Hall**
"Cyril"
Died 17th September
1968
aged 74 years
Loves last gift
remembrance

Also his beloved wife
Edith
Roseanna
Died 17th Dec
1978
aged 93 years
Reunited

F246A

Slab

Lacey William
Creed
Died
16th March 1963
aged 71 years

F247A

Open book

In loving memory of
Douglas
Magub
Died
July 3rd
1972
Aged 92

Ninette
Magub
Died
April 3rd
1973
Aged 91

F248A

Open book

In loving
memory of
Donald
Stewart
Died 10. May
1965
aged 54
At rest

Also
his wife
Eleanor
Ninette
Died 11th March
1998
aged 83
Re-united

F249A

Open book

In loving
memory of
**Ruby May
Stewart**
Died 29 Sept.
1966
aged 48

F250A

Open book

In loving   Died
memory of   30th May
Leonard   1968
Harry   aged 77
Phillips   *At rest*

F251A

Slab

In loving memory of
Sydney Maurice Spaull
Died 12th April 1967
one time organist
of this church

F252A

Open book

In loving   And of
memory of   his wife
Arthur Sydney Smith **Lilian**
Major   **Mary Smith**
Indian Army   **neé Finch**
Born Dec. 5   Born Mar. 18
1902   1896
Died Dec. 31   Died Feb. 8
1967   1973
One short sleep   *And death shall*
past we wake eternally *be no more*

F253A

Divided stone

Adolphus
James Askew
aged 79 years
who died 24th July 1977
*Together again for
eternity*

In loving memory of
Nettie Ada Askew
aged 71 years
who died 23rd Jan. 1970
A wonderful wife
and mother

F254A

Open book

**William Wallace
Turner**
Died 8th March
1969
aged 78 years
At rest

**Lillie
Turner**
Died 7th July
1979
aged 82 years
Reunited

F255A

Open book on
plinth with
plaque in front

In loving
memory of
Dora Frizzell
Died
21st Jan. 1969
aged 58

Also
**Alan Fitzroy
Frizzell**
Died
6th Sept. 1973
aged 65

In loving memory of
a dear husband
and father
Robert G. Frizzell
1936 – 1983

F256A

In
loving memory of
Eliza Story Thompson
who died May 9th 1964
in her 93rd year
And of
John William Thompson
who died March 28th 1948
in his 84th year

The modern terracotta plaque in the style of the 19th century Harmer panels

SECTION G

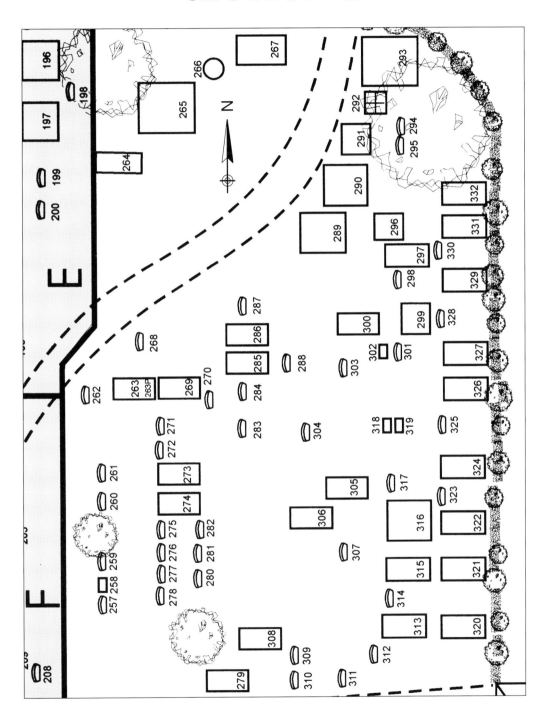

SECTION G
G257 – 332

G257

Headstone

In memory
of **Elizabeth** daughter
of Jeremiah French who died Nov. [7th] 1750
aged 5 years

G258

Open book

In loving
memory of
**Thomas
Chatfield**
died 3rd Aug.
1918
aged 74

Also **Emma**
his wife
died 13th July
1935
aged 88
At rest

G259

Headstone

In loving memory of
Louisa
eldest daughter of
Thomas and Emma Chatfield
who died on her birthday
June 20th 1887
aged 18 years
*Blessed are they that mourn for they
shall be comforted*

G260

Headstone

To the memory of
Jeremiah French
who departed this life
17th Sept. 1763 aged 55 years
Also of **John** son of
Jeremiah and Eliz. French
who died 10th September 1761
aged 17 years

G261

Headstone

To the memory of
Mary French daughter
of Jeremiah & Elith French
who died 17th Nov. 1771
aged 39 years

G262

Headstone

William James Gifkins
died March 20th 1883
aged 8 years 7 months
He shall gather the lambs
with his arms and carry them
in his bosom

G263

Kerb

In memory of **John Grant** who died January 24th 1937
aged 79 years

G263P

Plaque

In
loving memory
of
Albert Hall
who died
September 15th 1884
aged 35 years

G264

Kerb and cross

Caroline Anne Langdale
Born June 3rd 1840 died June 15th 1887
I will lay me down in peace and take my rest
Resting

G265

Pink polished
granite cross
with three steps
and stone kerb.
Iron railings
missing

Sophia Clements
wife of Henry Topham Clements
of Belmont, East Hothly
Born December 25th 1837
Died July 23rd 1904
Them also which sleep in Jesus
will God bring with him   1 Thes. IV. 14
In love, in faith, in hope
To **Caroline Sarah**
wife of
Henry Topham Clements
of Belmont in this parish
Born 10th May 1833
Died 11th April 1886
Fear not for I have redeemed thee, I have called
Thee by thy name; thou art mine Isa. XLIII. 1
Also to
Henry Topham Clements
of Belmont in this Parish
Born 15th December 1830
Died 8th October 1900
Captain late of the 13th and 14th
Kings Lt. Dragoons
In the latter Regt. he served as
Adjt. in the expedition to Persia and
throughout the Indian Mutiny 1857 – 8 – 9
Remember me, O my God for good Nehemiah XIII. 31
Also to
two of their children who were
born and died at Belmont
Caroline Mary
Born 1st Decr. 1867. Died 15th Jany. 1868
Edward Lucius Topham
Born 31st August 1866 died 7th June 1869

G266*

Rocks with metal plaque

In loving memory
of
**Frances Evelyn Swann
(neé Harbord)**
1887 - 1954
Stephen Gordon Harbord
1890
Killed in action 1917
Geoffrey Mann Harbord
1892 - 1953
Ellen Beatrice Marian Harbord
1894 - 1942

* Note – The Parish Burials Registers state that the ashes of **Geoffrey Mann Harbord** are buried in the grave of Morag E. Harbord. There is no record of a Morag Harbord buried in the churchyard.

G267

Polished red granite cross on 4 tiers and kerb

In
loving memory
of
Henrietta Maples
wife of Francis Maples
Born 29th November 1839
Died 29th January 1928

G268

Scrolled headstone

In
loving
memory of
**Susannah Gorringe
Benham**
who died 3rd August
1890 aged 47
daughter of George
and Susannah Benham
Looking unto Jesus

G269

Kerb

In ever loving memory of **Sarah Hall**
who fell asleep September 24th 1932 aged 82
Weep not, she is not dead but sleepeth

G270

Headstone

In
loving memory
of
Kate Wheeler Pelham
who died February 12th 1891
aged 1 year and 8 months
Safe in the arms of Jesus

G271

Headstone

In memory of
Harriett
wife of Richard Grant
Born January 19th 1819
died February 17th 1866
Also of
Rachel Grant
daughter of the above
Born October 7th 1848
Died March 21st 1867

G272

Headstone

In memory of
Richard Grant
Born 24th April 1821
Died 12th December 1893
Also of **Ruth Hall**
granddaughter of the above
Died 28th October 1927
aged 53 years
Underneath are the everlasting arms

G273*

Tomb

Sacred to the memory of
Mr. Joseph Fuller
late of Waldron
who departed this life Nov. 4th 1806
aged 76 years
also of **Mrs. Ann Fuller** his wife
who died the 2nd August 1811
aged 78 years
Sacred to the memory of
Mr. Joseph Fuller
Formerly of Mays in this County
who died the 2nd March 1845
aged 75 years

Also of **Mrs. Eliza**[bth] **Fuller** his wife
who died 25th December 1856
aged 86 years
**Mr. Joseph Paine
Fuller**
son of Joseph and
Elizabeth Fuller
died 10th January
1843
aged 33 years

Note – Mays is a house in Selmeston

G274

Tomb

To the memory of
Mrs. Mary Paine (wife
of Mr. Nathaniel Paine
Surgeon of this Parish)
who died April the 1st 1773
aged 26 years
Also of the above named
Nathaniel Paine
who died July 5th 1807
aged 64 years
Mary daughter of
Nathaniel and Mary
Paine Died March
the 23rd 1776 aged 6
years
John
Son of Nathaniel
and Mary Paine
died March the 2nd
1776 aged 4
years

G275

Headstone

In loving memory
of
Sarah Jane Norman
daughter of
Henry and Hannah Norman
who departed this life
16th February 1870
aged 13 years
Thy will be done

G276

Headstone

In memory of
William Terry
who departed this life
August 4th 1863
aged 70 years
Also of **Hannah** his wife
who died August 13th 1869
aged 75 years

G277

Headstone

To the memory
of **Mrs. Sarah Adams**
who died May 8th 1774
in the 83rd year of her
age

G278

Headstone

In
ever loving memory
of
John William Cosham
the beloved husband of
Annie Cosham
who passed away Nov. 20th 1918
aged 38 years
At Rest
Also in loving memory
of
Annie Cosham
who passed away May 25th 1972
in her 90th year
Re-united

G279

Headstone
and kerb

In memory of
a dearly loved husband and "Daddy"
Frank Henry Burfield
who died 13th March 1950
aged 48 years
Loves last gift - remembrance
Edith Sylvia Ades
10 Mar. 1913 – 22 Oct. 1997
*Forever in our
thoughts*

G280

Headstone

In memory of
John Davis
late of this Parish
who died 12th December
MDCCCLIV
aged 82 years
Our hearts are fastened to the world,
By strong and various ties
But every sorrow cuts a string,
And urges us to rise
But you are washed in Jesu's blood
and thus prepared to die
His blood alone gives peace with God,
and ripens for the sky
The Saviour yet invites you all
To knock at mercy's gate
Arise, arise for mercy call,
before it be too late

G281

Headstone

Near this place lies interr^d
the body of **Josias Smith**
of this Parish
who departed this life
July the 31st 1736
in the seventieth year of his age
Also **Elizabeth** his wife
who departed this life
December ye 13th 1761
in the seventy eight
year of her age

G282

Headstone

In memory
of
Anne Norman
daughter of
Henry and Hannah Norman
who departed this life
5th October 1873
aged 19 years
Blessed are the pure in heart
for they shall see God

G283

Headstone

In memory of
Jemima
the beloved wife of
Samuel Watford
who died July 10th 1868
aged 76 years
Also of
Samuel Watford
who died Decr. 10th 1869
aged 80 years

G284

Shaped cros

Not lost but gone before
In loving memory of
Frederick Watford
who died April 22nd 1880
aged   25 years
In the midst of life we are in death

G285

Headstone with
footstone and kerb

In affectionate remembrance
of
George Watford
(of this Parish)
who fell asleep Janry 29th 1885
in the 66th year of his age
In the midst of life we are in death
Also of **Barbara** his wife
who died June 10th 1859
aged 40 years
And of **Ellen** their youngsest daughter
who died April 20th 1853
aged 4 months
(Footstone – G.W. 1885 B.W. 1859   E.W. 1853)

G286

Flat slab,
railings missing

Sacred
to the memory of
General George Rees Kemp
of her Majesty's Indian Army
Colonel of the 22nd Regiment
Bombay Native Infantry
who died
at his residence Spring Lodge
in this Parish
on the 16th of September 1861
deeply regretted
Also of **Ann** his wife
who died Feb. 9th 1875
at Spring Lodge
in her 83rd year

G287

Headstone

In loving memory of
George Benham, Esq.,
Late a commissioned officer
H.M. Customs, London
12 years a resident of this Parish,
born in North Devon
Septr. 9th 1807
Died May 3rd 1879
Christ saith I am the resurrection
and the life
Also **Susannah neé Goring**
wife of the above
a member of the old Sussex
County family of that name
Born in London
Febry 22nd 1820
Died Febry 23rd 1888
They will rise again

G288

Headstone

Sacred to the memory of
Thomas Booker
late of Halland
who died September 12th 1884
aged 77 years
Also of **Sarah** his wife
who died July 14th 1865
aged 56 years
Also of **Anne** their daughter
who died January 3rd 1857
aged 22 years
Blessed are the dead which die in the Lord

G289*

elaborate column
with cross; column
flanked by four
angels

The
Family
Grave
of
**Joseph
Rickett**
of
Barham

Joseph Rickett
Born April 29th 1819
Died Jan. 24th 1892
*With Christ
which is
far better*

Cordelia wife of
Percy M. Stewart
Born Oct. 18th 1871
Died Sept. 28th 1906
daughter of
J. Compton and
Catherine S. Rickett
*She openeth her
mouth with wisdom
and
in her tongue is
the law of kindness*

**Cordelia
Jane
Rickett**
Born
23rd June 1826
Died
Nov. 4th
1896
*Her life is written
in
the living letters
of
her children's love*

In memory of
**Charles Stuart
Rickett, M.A.**
youngest son of
Joseph & Cordelia
Rickett
who died June 4th 1883
in his 26th year
*"He hath given me rest
by his sorrow and
life by his death*

Richard Allen Compton
son of Richard and Catherine Emily Ho[lmes]
Born Sept. 17th 1895
died Aug. 5th 1896

* Note – Catherine Emily Rickett, eldest daughter of J. Compton and Catherine Sarah Rickett, and granddaughter of Joseph and Cordelia Rickett, married the Rev. Richard Holmes. **Richard Allen Compton Holmes** was their first born who died aged 10 months. Joseph Rickett died of 'flu.

G293

Granite kerb and
stone cross

In loving memory of
Edward Langdale B.A.
54 years Rector of this Parish
Born May 15th 1802
Died January 27th 1882
"And when the chief Shepherd shall
appear ye shall receive a crown of
glory that fadeth not away. Peter V 4
Also
Emily Mary Langdale
his wife
Born March 12th 1816
Died April 26th 1883
Then are they glad because
they are at rest and so He
bringeth them unto the haven
where they would be. Psalm CVII. 30

———————

G294

Headstone

In
loving memory of
Robert Knight
late Rector of Southleigh
who died 4th May 1923
aged 83 years
and of
Emily Joyce Knight
his beloved wife
who died 12th May 1924
in her 83rd year
Them also that sleep in Jesus
will God bring with him I Thes. 4. 14

———————

G295

Headstone

In memory of
Janet Constance
Harbord
Born September 21st 1884
Died September 24th 1884
Florence Kathleen Harbord
Born December 13th 1885
Died June 5th 1889
"Is it well with the child?" "It is well"

G290

Large cross,
kerb with railing
and two small
crosses at the foot

Here rests the body of
Harry Harbord, M.A.
Died May 10 1920
aged 76
32 years Rector of this Parish
Also of **Ellen Jane** his wife died May 4th 1927 aged 69

G291

Square splinth,
tall column
with cross

Sacred
to the memory of
Elizabeth Langdale
Born 12th March 1791
Died 17th Oct. 1857
Also
Charlotte Langdale
Born 3rd January 1799
Died 1st March 1863

G292

Small cross
on plinth

Sacred
to the memory of
Mary Langdale
Born June the 8th 1793
Died May the 28th 1869
Also
Ann Lucy Langdale
Born 3rd February 1896
Died 2nd July 1871

G296

Elaborate
memorial

Sacred
to the memory of
William Gilliat,
of Barham
who fell asleep in Jesus
March 27th 1868
aged 77
He being dead yet speaketh
Heb. 11. 4
Sacred
to the memory of
The Revd. Henry Robinson, M.A.
Priest of the Church of God
Vicar of Westfield , Sussex
son-in-law of William Gilliat
who fell asleep in Jesus
on the eve of All Saints
October 31st 1888
aged 69
Also in memory of
Elizabeth wife of the
Revd. Henry Robinson
and daughter of
William and Sophia Gilliatt
who fell asleep Aug. 12 1903
aged 30 years
One family we dwell in Him
One church above beneath

Note - There is a plaque missing from the side of this memorial which probably commemorated **Sophia Gilliat**, wife of William, who was buried 11th December 1866 aged 66

G297

Kerb and low
headstone

In
affectionate remembrance of
a dear daddy
Ernest A. Pankhurst
aged 45 years
Died 3rd Nov. 1948

G298

Headstone

In
loving memory of
**Bernard James
Croft**
adopted son of
C. and D. Keeley
who died 12th Feb. 1948
aged 21 years
*In the midst of life,
we are in death*

G299

Kerb and
headstone

In loving memory
of

**Peter Richard   Gordon George
Starnes   Heasman**

Died Dec. 7th 1946 aged 19 years
*Lovely and pleasant in their lives and in their
death they were not divided
For God so loved the world that he gave his only
begotten son, that whosoever believed in Him should
not perish, but have everlasting life*

G300

Headstone

In
loving memory of
Mary Beatrice Knight
who died December 31st 1946
aged 72 years
Rest in Peace
Also of her husband
Frank Knight
who died November 23rd 1948
aged 80 years
From all their labours now they rest

G301

Headstone

Sacred
to the memory of
Emma Elizabeth
wife of
George Burnell
Died April 29th 1860
aged 36

G302*

Shield shaped
plaque

In
loving memory of
Catherine
M. Ranger
Died March 9th 1945
Also of **Charles P. Ranger**
Died July 23rd 1949
In heavenly
love abiding

* Note – This plaque is leaning against another gravestone and does not mark the actual burial place

---

G303

Headstone

Sacred
to the memory of
Samuel Holman
late of this Parish
who departed this life on
the 6th day of April 1833
aged 66 years
Also of **Elizabeth** his wife
who died the 11th June 1838 aged 74 years
Blessed are they and only they
when in the Lord their saviour die
Their bodies wait redemptions day
and sleep in peace where'er they lie

G304

Headstone

In memory
of
Ellen
youngest daughter of the late
Samuel Watford
of this Parish
who died February 19th 1895
aged 63 years
Also of
Mary his eldest daughter
who died October 7th 1896
aged 69 years
With Christ which is far better Phil. I. 23

G305

Headstone
and kerb

In
loving and grateful memory
of
our dear mother
Emily Finnegan
who died 19th February 1950
aged 82 years

G306

Headstone
and kerb

In
loving memory of
Richard Hunnisett
who died 19th Jan. 1930
aged 91 years
Also of
Mary his wife
who died 28th Octr. 1905
aged 64 years

G307

Headstone

In loving memory of
John Pentecost Hunnisett
who died April 22nd 1882
aged 12 months
Also of
Rosina Jessie Hunnisett
who died Decr. 19th 1882
aged 6 weeks
Jesus said suffer little children
to come unto Me and forbid them
not for of such is the kingdom
of heaven
Luke 18. 16

G308

Kerb and
heastone

Jesu Mercy
In
loving memory
of
Frances Rosella Mary
wife of William Mylius
who departed this life 28th Janry 1882
aged 23 years
So He giveth his beloved sleep

G309

Headstone and
footstone

In memory of
kind and affectionate parents
Edmund Parris
of this Parish
who departed this life
April 3rd 1871
aged 67 years
"Come unto me all ye that labour
and are heavy laden and I will give
you rest Matt: XI 28
Also of
Sarah Ann his wife
who departed this life
Janry. 16th 1873
aged 60 years
"Behold God is my salvation I will
trust, and not be afraid" Isaiah XII 2.
(Footstone – E.P. 1871 S.A.P. 1873)

G310

Headstone

In loving memory
of
Hannah
the beloved wife of
John Haizelden
of Wandsworth, Surrey
who fell asleep January 10th 1889
aged 22 years
Sorrow not even as others which have no hope
for if we believe that Jesus died and rose
again, even so them also which sleep in Jesus
will God bring with Him
Wherefore comfort one another with these words
I The. IV 13. 14. 18.
Also of **Sarah Parris**
sister of the above
Died Oct. 11th 1947
aged 82
He Knoweth them that trust in him
Nahum I. 7

G311

Headstone

Here rests
dearly loved parents
Rebecca Parris
died 7th Sept. 1880
aged 46
John Parris
died 16th March 1925
aged 88
The Lord gave and hath taken
Hallowed be his name
And
Edward their eldest son
died 8th April 1868
aged 10

G312

Headstone

In
loving memory
of
Harriett Funnell
died 7th Aug 1946
aged 85 years
Also of her husband
Herbert Funnell
died 10th February 1947
aged 84 years

G313

Headstone

Group Captain
J. Goodhart
Royal Air Force
21st January 1944 age 34
Lovely and pleasant
in their lives
and in their death
they were not divided
His wife, son
and mother-in-law
Christabel Alice
age 43
Michael John
age 9
Alice Maud Smith
age 67
All killed by enemy action
Jan. 21st 1944

G314

Headstone

In loving memory of
Rowland Burfield
died June 16th 1945
aged 78 years
Also of his wife **Emma**
died January 13th 1950
aged 81 years
Gone from us but not forgotten
never shall their memory fade
sweetest thoughts shall ever linger
around the spot where they are laid

121

G315

Kerb

In loving memory of a dear husband and father
Charles French died April 24th 1945
Also of a devoted wife and mother **Ruth French**
died June 12th 1952 aged 82 years
In thy presence is
fullness of joy

G316

Double sided
headstone
and kerb

Naomi Mathews
who died 30th March 1888
aged 52 years
"In returning and rest shall ye be
saved
In quietness and in confidence
shall be your strength" Isaiah XXX 15
Also of **Mary Matilda**
daughter of Charles Henry
and Naomi Mathews
of Halland
who died 26th May 1893
aged 21 years
Tell them to seek Jesus

Sacred to the memory
of
Annie
the second beloved wife of
Charles Henry Mathews
who passed into the better land
on the 26th December 1930,
aged 93 years and 9 months
How sweet to be loved of the lovely one
The Song of Songs V.16
Also of **Charles Henry Mathews**
for 46 years Minister of the Gospel
at Halland
who peacefully passed to his
eternal rest on February 24th 1932,
aged 92 years and 8 months
Faithfull unto death Rev. II. 10

G317

Double sided
headstone

Samuel Elgar Durrant
died 1st October 1867
aged 36 years
I have loved thee with all everlasting
love; therefore with loving kindness
have I drawn thee unto me

Sacred
to
the memory of
Louis Johnson
Durrant
who died at Queensland
1869
aged 25 years

G318A

Plaque

Frederick William
Haynes
Died 24th October 1992
aged 76 years

G319A

Plaque

Our dear mother
Emily Laura Haynes

G320

Kerb

Loving remembrance of my dear husband **Edwin Veners**
departed this life June 4 1928 aged 55 years
R.I.P.

G321

Kerb

In loving memory of **John Frederick Knight**
who died October 5 1942 aged 81
Also of **Sarah Jane Knight** who died April 2nd 1951 aged 88

G322

Kerb

In loving memory of
Edith Augusta Mitchell
a servant of Christ 27 Nov. 1856 29 Jan 1945

G323

Headstone

In
loving memory of
Emma Bishop
died 13.2.45
aged 77 years
Also of **Edward**
husband of the above
Died 3.5.63
aged 96 years
Reunited

G324

Kerb

In loving memory of
John Cosham died April 8th 1925 aged 69
Also of **Mary Ann** his beloved wife died April 24th 1926
aged 65 years

G325

Headstone

In ever loving memory
of
John Pentecost Hunnisett
who passed away 30th Novr. 1878
aged 33 years
*Jesus said I am the resurrection and
the life He that believeth in Me though
he were dead yet shall he live*
Also of his wife
Emily
who fell asleep 3rd Feby. 1925
aged 75 years
*Whosoever liveth and believeth in Me
shall never die*

G326

Kerb

Mary Louisa Trussler died Nov. 11 1948 aged 72 years
Harry George Trussler died May 28th 1951 aged 81 years

G327

Kerb

In loving memory of **Sidney James Hall**
Died 10th December 1948 aged 86
In the garden of memories we meet every day.
Also **Laura Rachel Hall** died 10th May 1970 aged 88
Reunited

G328

Headstone

Sacred
to the memory
of
William Guy
who died Dec. 28th 1868
aged 76 years
Also of **Ann** his wife,
who died May 22nd 1869
aged 70 years
*Blessed are the dead who die in the
Lord*

G329

Kerb

In loving memory of **Elmer Heppy de Voil**
who fell asleep Feb. 9th 1949
Also of her husband **Charles Walter de Voil**
who fell asleep Feb. 17 1954 aged 83
*Father in Thy gracious keeping
leave we now thy servant sleeping*

G330

Headstone

Sacred
to the memory of
Ellen Fitzherbert
the beloved child
of George and Elizabeth
Langdon
of Kemp Town, Brighton
who departed this life
October 26th 1850
aged 4 years
"Of such is the Kingdom of God"

G331

Tomb

Sacred
to the memory of
Ellen
the beloved wife of
Robert William Cumberbatch
of Chiddingly in this county
who departed this life
the [XIXth] of March MDCCCXLV
in the XXXII year of her life

G332

Tomb

To the memory of
Elizabeth wife of
the Reverend
Edward Rudstone Langdale
who died June 4th 1836
aged 76
To the memory
of
Emily Elizabeth
daughter of
Edward & Emily Mary
Langdale
who died Oct. 16th 1837
aged 6 months
To the memory of
the Reverend
Edward Rudstone Langdale M.A.
Rector of this Parish
Thirty five years
who died February 16th 1838
aged 83
To the memory
of
Edward infant son
of
Edward & Emily Mary
Langdale
who died Sept. 5th
1838

SECTION H

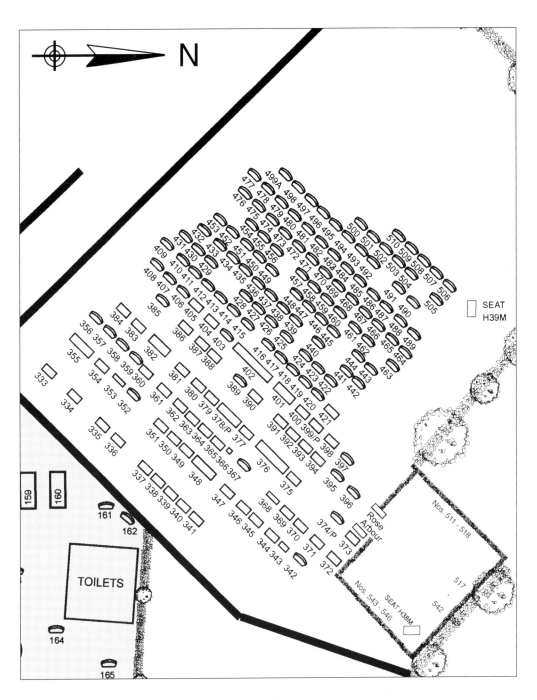

H333

Slab

Amy
Macrae
December 1865
November 1949

———

H333P

Vase

Catherine Sutton

———

H334

Kerb

In loving memory of
Emily Betsy Beeny fell asleep 6th December 1958 aged 78

———

H335

Inset Slab

In loving
memory of
Albert Edward Benney
1881 – 1950

———

H336

Headstone
and kerb

In
loving memory
of
Frank Howard
Died 10th Jany 1951
aged 83
Rest in Peace

H337

Red granite kerb

Alfred Percy Hoare
who fell asleep 22nd March
1951
aged 69 years
Look back and give thanks
Look forward and take courage

H338

In the loving memory of
George Marchant
Died January 18th 1951 aged 61
God takes our loved ones from our homes
but never from our hearts
And of his beloved wife
Violet May
Died August 12th 1969 aged 73
Resting

H339

Kerb

George Quested who died 20th January 1951 aged 62
Also of our son **Connell** killed in Burma 22nd May 1943
aged 24
Also of his dear wife **Kate** died 25th July 1969
Re-united

H340

Kerb

Edith Jane Crowhurst 25.2.1951
George Owen Crowhurst 18.5.1954
Treasured memories of our dear parents
Re-united

H341

Kerb

In memory of
a beloved wife **Mary Ann Turner** died 21st March 1951
aged 73 years
Also **Stanley Turner** died 3rd Apl. 1964 aged 78

H342*

Headstone

Liam Michael
Catt
31st Dec. 1994
Forever in our thoughts

★Note – **Liam Michael Lawrence** in Burials Register

H343

kerb

Marion Frances Thomas *God's gift*
Taken 21st Nov. 1956 aged 19 days

H344

Headstone with
inset anvil

In memory of
Rodney
Cruttenden
Died 21st July 1953
aged 71 years
Gone but not forgotten

H344P

Open book

In loving
memory of
"Stib"
Stephen
Ernest
Ades

Died
6th Dec.
1965
aged
56 years
At Rest

H345

Headstone
and kerb

In loving memory of
a dear husband and father
Charles Carey
passed away 7th February 1953
aged 36 years
In the garden of memory we meet every day
At Rest

H346

Headstone and
kerb

In
loving memory of
Nellie Moore
Died 28th January 1953
aged 77 years

———

H347

Kerb

In loving memory of
our dear parents
Sylvia Susetta Burchett
Died 28th April 1951
aged 61 years
Ernest Robert Burchett
Died 21st December 1955
aged 66 years
Re-united

———

H348

Kerb

In loving memory of a devoted husband and father
George Westgate, died 25th July 1951 aged 78 years
In loving memory of a devoted husband
Walter Westgate died 10th September 1951 aged 39 years
Also **Harriet Westgate** died 17th March 1954 aged 80 years
Re-united
Also **Annie Westgate** died 6th April 1954 aged 63 years

———

H349

Granite Kerb

In loving memory of our dear old friend **Agnes Hillier**
who died 17th March 1952 aged 87 years
Also **Minnie Hillier** died 7th Feb. 1952 aged 86 years
Cremated at Brighton
Peace
With Christ
which is far better

———

H350

Kerb

In loving memory of
Edward Thomas Novis died 22nd January 1953 aged 71 years
Harriett Maud Novis died 7th June 1954 aged 74 years
At rest

H351

Kerb

In loving memory of
a dear mother
Julia Thurgood
Died 18th Nov. 1952
aged 75

H352

Headstone

In loving memory
of
George Arrow Lambert
who died October 23rd 1951
aged 69 years
and **Hilda Mary Lambert**
who died October 6th 1984
aged 84 years

H353

Inset slab

In loving memory
of
a dear husband and father
Ernest L. Brooks
Died 7th Octr. 1951
aged 72 years
Also a dear wife and mother
Harriott J. Brooks
Died 9th Novr. 1969
aged 81 years

H354

Headstone
and kerb

In loving memory of
Elsie Martha Venner
who died 30th August 1951
aged 58
At peace
Also of her husband
John Frank Venner
who died 3rd September 1963
aged 62 years
Peace perfect peace

H355

Kerb

Edith Caroline, beloved wife of Alfred G. Howard
Died 12th April 1951 aged 80 years
Resting in peace
Alfred Gravely Howard died 17th Oct. 1951 in his 90th year
Their spirit liveth

H356

Headstone

Sacred
to the memory
of
a wonderful father
Harold William
Pearson
who passed to rest
29th July 1957
aged 79 years

H357

Plaque

Fond memories of
our dear brother
Freddie Burchett
At rest
Nov. 16th 1955
aged 72
Will. Walt (Canada)
& Annie

H358

Headstone

In loving
memory of
Sarah Emily
Robinson
passed over
November 3rd 1955
*"Underneath are
the everlasting
arms"*

H359

Headstone

In
loving memory of
**Reginald Frederick
Turner**
aged 63
Also his wife
Edith
aged 81
Always in our thoughts

H360

Kerb

In memory of
Sidney Charles Turner died April 5 1955 aged 76
Also of his wife **Mary Turner**
Died March 11th 1963 aged 83
Re-united

H361

Headstone
and kerb

In
loving memory of
Elvina
wife of Thomas Edward Fuller
and dear mother of seven children
Died April 3rd 1955 aged 82

H362

Kerb

Amy G. Hunnisett died 30th March 1955 aged 46 years *At rest*
Also of her father **Albert Hunnisett** died 19th October 1955
aged 80years
And her mother **Mary Jane Hunnisett** died 8th May 1959
aged 72 years

H363

Headstone
and kerb

In
loving memory of
Sidney Eade
died 25th Mar. 1955 aged 80
Also of his beloved wife
Lily Eade
Died 31st August 1958 aged 82

H364

Headstone
and kerb

Resting
In loving memory of
Ida Cassy Guy
who died 18th January 1955
aged 69 years
One of the best
And
Walter William Guy
who died 4th October 1967
aged 84 years
Re-united

⋇═══════════⋇

H365

Kerb

In loving memory of **Thomas Henry Carley**
who died 24th November 1954 aged 63 years

⋇═══════════⋇

H366*

No inscription. Metal Marker no. 25

*Note – This is possibly the grave of **Reginald Ernest Marant**, who died 19th July 1954 aged 58.

⋇═══════════⋇

H367

Headstone

In loving memory of
**Wilfred Cecil
Corke**
Died 1st July 1954
aged 36 years
At rest

⋇═══════════⋇

H368

Headstone
and kerb

In loving memory of
a devoted wife
Minnie Stepney
who died 23rd February 1954
aged 50 years
Till we meet again
Also **Charles Stepney**
Died 21st July 1972
aged 67 years

H369

Headstone

In loving memory of
a dear wife and mother
Martha Ruth Chatfield
Died 24th September 1953 aged 62 years
At rest
Also of a devoted husband and father
William Thomas Chatfield
Died 19th March 1962 aged 80 years
Re-united

H370

Kerb

In loving memory of **Emily Starnes** died 3rd February 1954
aged 77 years
Also of her husband **Frederick Starnes**
Died 15th June 1956 aged 76 years
*I will come again and receive
you unto myself John 14.3*

H371

Headstone
and kerb

Sleeping
In loving memory of
our dear parents
John Dunstone Burtenshaw
Died 2nd Feb. 1954
aged 70 years
Annie Harriett Burtenshaw
Died 31st May 1955
aged 72 years
Re-united

H372

Headstone

In
loving memory
of
our sister
Florence Wright
Died 31st January 1954
aged 54

H373

Kerb

Helen Kate Thomson died 20th July 1958 aged 85

———————————————

H374

Kerb

In
loving memory of
my dear husband
**John Frederick
Kemp**
Died Oct. 3rd 1956
aged 62 years

———————————————

H375

Headstone
and kerb

In loving memory of
**Esther Maude
Freshwater**
who died 10th October 1955
aged 55 years
*God takes our loved ones
from our homes but never
from our hearts*
Also of
her husband and our dear father
Arthur Freshwater
who died 20th February 1968
aged 74 years
Re-united

———————————————

H375P

Plaque

Also of their son
Donald Arthur
Died 11th Feb. 1979
aged 54
Called to rest

———————————————

H376

Kerb

James Garland
1889 – 1955
Gertrude Garland
1890 – 1975

H377

Kerb

In loving memory of
William Alfred Goldsmith
Died 7th November 1955 aged 72
Also of **Amelia** his wife who died 16th September 1968
aged 90 years

H378

Kerb

In loving memory of
my dear wife **Florence Minnie Rich** died 5th March 1956
aged 64 years
Thy will be done
Also of her devoted husband **Robert Walter Rich**
died 21st March 1964 aged 73 years
Re-united
Also **Ernest Robert Rich** elder son of Robert & Florence
Died 29th July 1979 aged 60 years

H379

Kerb

Kathleen Mary Starr April 29th 1956

H379P

Plaque

Constance Prescott
Died 3rd August 1992
aged 84 years

Mary-Claire de Courcy
6.5.1935 –
20.11.1997

H380

Kerb

In loving memory of **Edith Mary Playne**
19th May 1880 – 8th Jan. 1957
Also of **Mildred Lucetta Playne**
27th Nov. 1889 – 14th Aug. 1979

H381

Kerb

Samuel Holford Trill 1878 – 1957
Alice Ann Trill 1871 – 1958
Re-united

H382

Kerb

In loving memory of **Horace Edward Eade**
died Feb. 1st 1957 aged 82
In loving memory of **Esther Ellen Eade**
died March 25th 1980 aged 102
Peace, perfect peace

H383

Cross and kerb

In
loving memory
of
Dorothy Edith
wife of
Percy Ll. Hunting
of Old Whyly
1879 – 1958

H384

Cross and kerb

In
honoured and
loving memory
of
**Percy Llevellyn
Hunting**
Knight Bachelor
of Old Whyly
1885 – 1973

H385

Headstone

In loving memory of
**Cicely Margaret
Palmer**
who passed away
14th September 1962
aged 74 years
At peace

H386

Headstone and
kerb

In loving memory of my dear husband
Samuel Thomas Brown
who died 18th November 1959
aged 72 years
*God takes our loved ones from our
home but never from our hearts*
Also of his beloved wife
Ida Violet May Brown
who died 13th November 1972
aged 72 years
Re-united

H387

Kerb

In loving memory of **Emily** the wife of Frank Mitchell
died Oct. 8th 1959 aged 83
Also of **Frank Mitchell** died Oct. 30th 1961 aged 87

H388

Kerb

Doris Sarah French fell asleep Sept. 22nd 1959 aged 52
In God's keeping

H389

Headstone

In loving memory of
David Harold Jones
Died May 5th 1960
aged 53 years
Doris Evelyn Jones
Died Dec. 30th 1978
aged 68 years
Re-united

H390

Kerb and
open book

Sweet
memories of
Christine Ann
beloved only
daughter of
David and Evelyn
Jones
taken 8th Feb. 1959
Aged 12 years

*Her life is
a beautiful memory
her absence
a silent grief*

H391
Headstone

In
loving memory of
**Eleanor Julia
Press**
Passed over
Dec. 31st 1958
Rest in Peace

H392
Headstone

In loving
memory of a
devoted husband and father
Arthur Radley
Died 2nd November 1958
aged 71 years
*God takes our loved ones
from our homes but never
from our hearts*

H393
Headstone
and kerb

In loving memory of
Richard Howard Giles
Died 9th April 1958

H394
Kerb

A devoted wife and mother **Sarah Kate Driver**
Died 28th January 1959 aged 81 years
Also of a dear husband and father **Henry Driver**
Died 3rd August 1962 aged 87 years

H395
Headstone

In
loving memory
of
my dear husband
John Somerset
Died January 30th 1959
aged 71
Also his beloved wife
Henrietta
Died December 4th 1962
aged 71

141

H396

Headstone

In
loving memory of
Matilda Selina Durrant
who died 24th January 1960
aged 85 years
God takes our loved ones
from our homes but never
from our hearts
Also of her husband
Thomas Elgar Durrant
"Jimmy"
Re-united 19th April 1972
aged 91 years

H397

Headstone

In
memory of
Ernie Cosham
1961

H398

Kerb
(Masonic badge)

In the midst of life
we are in death
R.I.P.
In loving memory of
William Henry Thomas
Steel
Died 14th May 1965
aged 59 years

H399

Kerb

In loving memory of
Eva Minnie Steel
Died 5th Mar. 1960
aged 52 years
Also to the memory of
Harry Steel
Pilot Officer R.A.F.V.R.
Missing 12th Sept. 1940
aged 21 years

142

H399PA

Plaque

In loving memory
**Hazel Patricia
Arnold**
Died 18th June 1973
aged 61 years
Resting

H400

Kerb

In treasured memory
of a dear mother
and grandmother
Harriett Rebecca
wife of
William Wait Steel
Taken from us suddenly
January 13th 1970
in her 86th year

H400P

Open book

In loving
memory
**Hazel Patricia
(Pat) Steel**
1936 – 1986
Died 3rd October
Rest in peace
Many happy memories
Bill and the children

H401PA

Kerb

In loving memory of
**Stanley Alfred
Worsfold**
Died 26th October
1969
aged 48 years

**Keith John
Worsfold**
9.9.22 – 6.4.92
Dearly loved and
missed by us all

H401P

Open book

In loving memory of

Henry Worsfold
Died 20th June 1971
aged 83

Florence Violet Worsfold
Died 1st Oct. 1960
aged 70

Ever in our thoughts

H402P

Kerb

In loving memory of
Constance G. Coyle
Died 1st January 1965 aged 81 years
Loves last gift remembrance
Jessie Medcalf
Died 14th June 1966 aged 72 years
Harold Coyle
Died 19th January 1961 aged 78 years
Till we meet again

H403*

Open book

In loving memory of
Tony
beloved son of
Fred & Nellie
Mitchell
Died 26th Jan.
1962
aged 17 years

To live in the hearts of those we leave behind is not to die

*Note - **Anthony Steven Mitchell** in Burials Register

H404

Kerb

In loving memory of
Edward Charles Cosham
who died March 8th 1962
aged 65 years
Ever in our thoughts

H405

Kerb

In loving memory of
Walter Albert Kemp
who died 12th April 1962
aged 72 years
Also of **Mary Rose** his wife
Died 13th April 1973
aged 82

H406

Headstone

In
loving memory of
**Archie Atkinson
Clucas**
late of Ormskirk
Died 17th September 1962
aged 83 years
And his wife
Ann
Died 29th August 1966
aged 88 years

H407

Open book

Percy Edward Crowhurst	**Dorothy Mary Crowhurst**
called to rest Dec. 24th 1962	his wife called to rest Nov. 9th 1986

H408

Headstone

In
loving memory
of
**Florence
Lilian
Edwards**
Died
28th September 1971
aged 83 years
At rest

145

H409

Headstone

In
loving memory of
**Ernest Clement
Burton**
who died
July 18th 1971
aged 87 years

H410

Open book

In ever loving
memory of
**Winifred
Jenner**
Died
11th June 1966
aged 65 years
*Loves last gift
remembrance*

And
**Charles
Albert
Jenner**
Died
27th Jan. 1982
aged 78 years
Re-united

H411

Open book

In
loving
memory of
**Edith Bessie
Davies**
Born 9th Oct. 1920
Died 15th Aug. 1965
aged 44

*Father in thy
gracious keeping
leave we now
thy servant sleeping*

H411PA

Plaque

In loving memory of
my devoted wife
Mabel Keeley
Dec. 13th 1892 – Feb. 2nd 1970
and her husband
Clifford Robert Keeley
Oct 10th 1897 – Aug. 19th 1975

H412

Headstone

**Francis
(Frank)
Allen**
1908 – 1965
At rest

H413

Headstone

In
loving memory of
Gilbert Thomas Saunders
Died 5th July 1964
aged 38 years
Also of his mother
Ethel Annie Saunders
Died 16th June 1968
aged 76 years
At rest
And
Thomas Saunders
Died 28th March 1975

H414

Headstone

**Walter Cyril
Holman**
Born 6th October 1878
Died 29th December 1963

H415

Open book

Treasured memories of

**Nellie
Mitchell**
passed away
Jan. 30th 1963
aged 55 years
*For ever in
our thoughts*

**Fred
Mitchell**
Died on
March 16th 1984
aged 77 years
Re-united

H416

Open book

In
loving memory
of
**Ernest William
Hart-Cox**
who died
30th July 1963

And
of his wife
**Kathleen
Mary**
who died 28th Dec
1963

H417

Headstone

**Elizabeth
Lilian
Spencer**
1882 - 1963
At rest

H418

Open book

In loving
memory of
a dear mother
and sister
**Dorothy
Mary
Funnell**

Called to rest
27th April 1964
aged 44 years
*God takes our
loved ones from
our homes
but never from
our hearts*

H419

Headstone

In
loving memory of
Rhoda Betty Hyland
who died 14th October 1964
aged 45 years
"Thy will be done"

H420

Headstone

In
loving memory
of
our dear daughter
**Olwen Mary
Evenden**
Died 7th Feb. 1965
aged 41
Always in our thoughts

H421

Slab

In loving memory of
**Clifford Fortes
Loftus St. George**
C.B.E.
Born 22nd July 1894
Died 1st June 1966

H422

Open book

In
loving
memory of
Molly Jones
Died 12 Sept.
1971

Also
of her
husband
**Leslie
Jones**
Died 6th April
1976

H423

Headstone

In loving memory of
Dora Annie Peace
Died 25th November 1967
aged 76 years

H424

Headstone

In loving
memory of a devoted
husband & father
**Thomas Charles
Hazelden**
1901–1967
At rest

H425

Headstone

Loving memory of
Clement Evenden
Died 4th January 1968
aged 82 years
Till we meet again
Also of his dear wife
**Sarah Katherine
Evenden**
Died 20th December 1975
aged 83 years

H426

Open book

In loving
memory of
**Gertrude
Mary
Wickson**
who died
Feb. 28th 1968
aged 67 years
At rest

Also
**George
Henry
Wickson**
Died
Oct. 13th 1979
aged 80 years
Reunited

H427*

Metal Marker No. 32

*Note – There is no No. 32 in the Burials Register, therefore I have no name for this plot.

H428

Headstone

In loving memory of
a dear husband
father & grandfather
Bernard Arthur Pettit
Died April 2nd 1968
aged 78 years
Gone from us but not forgotten
Never shall thy memory fade
sweetest thoughts
shall ever linger
round this spot
where thou art laid
Also his wife
Ada Mary
Died Oct. 24th 1981
aged 90 years

H429

Open book

In loving
memory of
my dear wife
Emily Ada
Goldsmith
Died 22nd Nov. 1968
aged 80 years
God takes our
loved ones from
our homes but
never from our
hearts

Also
Walter
Goldsmith
1887–1978
Loved and
remembered

H430

Headstone

In loving memory
of
Margaret Ann Hickie
7.1.1893 – 26.12.1968
R.I.P

H431

Headstone

In loving memory of
**Benjamin Jabez
Baldock**
Died Oct. 12th 1969
Aged 87

———————

H432

Headstone

In
loving memory of
Charles Morley
of Graywood
who died
17th November 1972
aged 81 years

———————

H433

Headstone

In
loving memory of
my dear wife
Grace Bishop
Died July 7th 1971
Peace Perfect Peace
**Frederick Christopher
Bishop**
Passed away
Nov. 1st 1973
Rest in peace

———————

H434

Headstone

In loving memory of
Thomas Hugh Jones
Died March 26th 1971
Loved and remembered always

———————

H435

Open Book

In loving
memory of
**Lilian
Marian
Cole**

Died 21st August
1970

H436

Headstone

In memory of
**Marjorie Jewell
Greig**
a beloved wife and mother
1910 – 1970

H437

Open book

In
loving memory
of **Arthur Henry
Brooker**
Died April 1st 1970

In
loving memory
of
**Ada Clara
Brooker**
Died
May 15th 1972
aged 76

H438

Granite headstone

In
loving memory of
**Eva Louise
Ashdown**
who passed away
15th Jan. 1970

H439

Open book

In memory of
a dear husband
and father
**Herbert
Goldsmith**
Died
26th Oct. 1969
aged 78

Also of
a beloved wife
and mother
**Jessie L.
Goldsmith**
Died
18th Mar. 1981
aged 89

H440

Headstone

In
loving memory of
**Charles Mayes
Wigg**
Artist
1889-1969
Also
Roland Wigg
1893 – 1974
Beloved husband of Mary

H441

Plain cross with
one tier

In
loving memory
of
**Agnes Mildred
Birkett**
1880-1972

H442

Open book

In
loving
memory of
**Elizabeth
Goldsmith**

Died
21st May
1972
aged 88 years
At rest

H443

Headstone

In
ever loving memory of
a devoted wife and mother
Annie Amelia Ovenden
who died January 16th 1973
aged 75 years
Thomas Frank Ovenden
a dear husband and father
Died March 6th 1988
aged 89 years
Both sadly missed

H444

Cross on one tier

Evelyn Marion
Hunting
1888 – 1978
Widow of
Sir Percy Hunting
of Old Whyly
and sister of
Dorothy Hunting
and
Agnes Birkett

H445

Headstone

Treasured memories of
a beloved husband and father
Frank Nicholls
Died June 18 1974
"Abide with me"

H446

Headstone

In
loving memory
of
James Jeffery
Died 21st July 1974
aged 75 years

H447

Headstone

Lucy Nellie Gray
1888 – 1975
Dear friend
of the
Birkett & Hunting
families

H448

Open book

In loving
memory of
**Marion Ruby
Jobson**

Died
July 22nd 1975
aged 62

H449

Headstone

In loving memory of
George Knight
who died
10th November 1975
aged 67 years
In the garden of memory
we meet everyday
Also his wife
Florence Amy
Knight
who died
20th April 1978
aged 82 years
Together again

H450

Headstone

In
loving memory of
John C. Porter
Died 14th Nov. 1975
aged 68

H451

Open book

In loving
memory of
Harry
Victor
Barden
Died
19th Dec. 1975
aged 67 years
Till we meet again

Dorothy
Myrtle
Barden
nee Pettitt
died
2nd July 1978
aged 85 years

H452

White marker

Ray Salter

H453

Headstone

In
loving memory of
Ethel Rhoda
Wenham
Died 12th May 1977
aged 69 years

H454

Headstone

In
loving memory of
**Lois Elizabeth
Goldsmith
neé Bishop**
Died 15th June 1981
aged 86

H455

Headstone

In
loving memory
of
Edith West
who died May 11th 1981
aged 83 years

H456

Headstone

In loving memory of
a dear wife and mother
Margaret Irene Bassett
Born June 2 1908
Died Dec. 23 1980
Also
William James Bassett
Born Feb. 4 1906
Died March 15 1984
Both sadly missed

H457

Headstone

In loving memory
of
a much loved son
and brother
Michael Blunt
Died 23rd July 1979
aged 18
Always with us

H458

Plaque

In
loving memory of
**Ethel Eleanor
Durrant**
Died 12th Jan. 1979
aged 63 years

H459

Headstone

**Charles Thomas
Goldsmith**
1907–1979
Devoted husband
and father
So dearly loved
and
Amy Isabel
dear wife
of the above
1910–1989

H460

Headstone

In
loving memory of
William Edward Jeffery
Died 25th December 1978
aged 74 years
*Underneath are the everlasting
arms*
Also
in loving memory of
his wife
Lily May Jeffery
Died 23rd April 1994
aged 90 years
Sweet are the songs of Zion

H461

Headstone

In
loving memory of
**Albert Henry
Barlow**
1900-1978
and his wife
Doris Miriam
1901-1983

H462

Headstone

In ever
loving memory of
**Albertine Anna
Blaber**
who passed away
April 29th 1978
aged 65 years
A devoted wife and mother
So sadly missed
always in our thoughts
And
**John Edward
Blaber**
who passed away
December 17th 1987
aged 80 years
A loving husband and father
Rest in Peace
United once more

H463

Headstone

In
loving memory of
**John Henry
William Hylands
(Jack)**
25.5.1885 – 17.5.1977
Also his sister
**Beatrice May
Roffey**
17.6.1898 – 21.9.1983
At rest

159

H464

Headstone

James Francis
Joseph Anthony
Hanratty
Died 12th Feb. 1982
aged 67
To live in the hearts of
those we love is not to die
Jesus mercy   Mary help

H465

Headstone

In
loving memory of
a dear husband & father
Ian Harry Jolly
1948–1982
Forever in our thoughts

H466

Headstone

In loving
memory of a dear
husband & father
George Charles
Richards
1937–1982

H467

Headstone

In memory of
a loving wife
and devoted mother
Kathleen Florence Pettit
1913 - 1983
Also her dear husband
Eric Harold
1908 - 1987

H468

Headstone

Remembered
with love
Marjorie Doris Dade
1918 - 1983

H469*

Black polished
granite headstone
with gold lettering

In
loving
memory of
my dear wife
**Norah
Jeffery**
Born
27th August 1909
Died
4th April 1984

Also
of
her dear
husband
**Foreman
Jeffery**
Born
3rd July 1910
Died
30th August 1993

★ Note – Registered as **Elsie Agnes Norah Jeffery** and **Frederick George Jeffery** in the Burials Register

H470

Headstone

Nellie Burfield
1904 – 1984
**Nelson Edward John
Burfield**
1907 – 1989
Love's last gift remembrance

H471

Headstone

In
ever loving memory of
John James Shanks
Born 26 October 1906
Died 15 June 1985

H472

Headstone

In
loving memory of
Alfred (Roy) Allcorn
called to rest 28th September 1986
aged 77 years

H473

Headstone

In memory of
Sidney Foreman
"Sid"
1918 – 1986
R.I.P.

H474

Red granite
headstone

In
loving memory of
a dear wife & mother
Constance Marie Eade
7.7.1921 – 3.7.1987
Sadly missed
Reunited
With her husband
Edward Ypres Austin
Eade
4.5.1915 – 12.2.1998
Sadly missed father
and grandparents

H475

Headstone

Treasured memories of
a dear wife and mother
Ruby Baber
1909 – 1987
Also
a dear husband and father
Sydney Baber
(Pop)
1907 – 1991
Reunited

H476

Headstone

In memory of
**Joseph
William
Newman**
a much loved
father
and
grandfather
18.7.1901
29.12.1987

*Re-united
at last with*
**Sarah
nee Coffin**
beloved wife
and
mother
1.1.1904
16.6.1940

H477

Headstone

**John
Cruickshank**
of Belfast
Gentle scholar and mentor
1924-1995
Greatly loved

H478

Red granite
headstone

Cherished
memories of
a dear wife & mother
**Audrey Margaret
Stevens**
8.9.1936 - 17. 9. 1988
Abide with me

H479

Wooden cross

Jim Thompsett
15-8-41 - 6-6-91

H480

Heart shaped
headstone

Treasured memories
of our dear
little boy
**Jack Michael
Corke**
6.10.89 - 24.5.91
Forever in our thoughts

H481

Headstone

In loving memory of
Albert Harvey Miles
Captain Royal Navy
Died 13th May 1991
aged 87
And of
Joan Evelyn
his wife
Died 21 March 1992
aged 83

H482

Headstone

In loving memory
of
**William Stuart
Masters**
2nd June 1898
15th April 1991
R.I.P.

H483

Open book

In
loving
memory of
a dear
husband
and father
**Arthur
Edward
Pitman**
1920-1991

H484

Black granite
Headstone

Cherished
memories
of our dear Mum
**Gladys Muriel
Leigh**
1903-1989

H485*

Wooden plaque

17.11.4   28.8.89
Glynn Thomas Jenkins

★ Note – This wooden plaque was carved by Glynn's father.

H486

Heart shaped
headstone

Cherished memories
of our dearly loved
daughter
Joanna Kay Martin
25.5.84 – 11.5.89
Forever in our hearts

H487

Headstone

In loving memory of
a dear mother
and grandmother
**Muriel Dorothy Watkins
neé Stevens**
18th April 1916
13th April 1989

H488

Headstone

Cherished memories
of
Graham Deane
a dearly loved husband
and father
1921-1988

H489

Headstone

In
loving memory of
Jack Clark
1917 – 1988

H490

Headstone

**Melvyn
Humphrey**
11th March 1941
2nd December 1991
*A good friend
to so many*

———————

H491

Headstone

In
loving memory
of
**Isabel "Betty"
Duart**
25th November 1912
9th March 1992

———————

H492

Headstone

In loving memory
of
Dorothy M. Burchett
11.9.30 – 27.7.92
aged 61

———————

H493

Headstone

In
loving memory
Eric (Brub) Eade
1917 –1992

———————

H494

Headstone

In
loving memory
of
**Ernest George
Wenham**
Died Nov. 23rd 1993
aged 81 years

H495

Mr. Gurr
[and 1 other – name unknown]

H496

Headstone

In loving memory
of
a dear husband, dad
and granddad
George Sinden
Died 13th May 1994
aged 63 years
Forever in our thoughts

H497*

Headstone

Cherished memories
of our dear mother
Nellie Jones
Died aged 93 years
14th May 1994
and
our dear father
George Jones
Died aged 61 years
18th July 1961
In His care

H498*

Headstone

Treasured
memories of our loving and
courageous mother, darling
daughter, and great friend
**Shirley Christina Ann
Harrison**
14th May 1943 – 26th August 1993
The wind beneath our wings

★ Note – This headstone has an inset terracotta panel in imitation of the Harmer panels. It was made by Peartree Pottery, late of East Hoathly

167

H499A

Headstone

In loving memory
of
**Diane June
Farmer**
22nd June 1943
19th August 1991

H500

Headstone

In memory of
a loving wife and mother
Edith Mary Berry
aged 62 years

H501

Headstone

In
ever loving and treasured memories
of my dear husband
**Alan William David
Cottingham**
who departed this life
21 November 1996
aged 68 years
Loved with everlasting love

H502

Headstone

Rachel Wylie Logan
30.6.1915 – 21.7.1996

H503

Open book

In
loving
memory
of
a dear wife
and mother
Joan Smith
1919 –1996
*Forever in
our thoughts*

H504

Headstone

In
loving memory
of
Leonard William Oliver
19.7.1910 – 30.1.1996

H505

Wooden cross

Nicola Helen Clark

H506

Headstone

In remembrance of
Gladys Frances May Verrall
24.1.04 – 2.6.97
R.I.P.

H507

Headstone with
blue lettering

In loving memory
of
Edna Bedwell
1915 – 1998
*A light has gone
out from our lives*

H508

Headstone

In loving memory
of
Douglas Freear
2.10.1918 – 1.3.1998

H509

Headstone

Treasured memories
Of a dear husband
Father and grandfather
Robert Charles Hart
19th February 1918 – 20th April 1998
He was a kind man

H510

Jack Barden

H511

**Henry Herbert
Thomas Allen**
Died 6th May 1994
aged 95 years

H512

**Anthony George
Bergen Gander**
Died 27th March 1984
aged 65 years

H513

**Noreen Mary
Bradford**
Died 16th July 1985
aged 75 years

H514

**Nellie Muriel
Barden**
Died 5th December
1986
aged 69 years

H515

**Olive Maude
Thorpe**
Died 21st June 1987
aged 66 years

**Philip James
Thorpe**
Died 30th September 1987
aged 69 years

H516

**Gordon
Gibson**
Died 4th February 1989
aged 69 years

**Irene Elsie
Gibson**
Died 31st August 1992
aged 70 years

H517

**Charles
Strong**
Died 24th April 1985
aged 72 years

H518

**Annie Kathleen
Waller Routh**
Died 13th February 1985
aged 91 years

H519

In memory
Ronald Brown
1907–1998

H520

**Marion Louise
Meakin**
Died 20th January 1985
aged 75 years

H521

Lynn Abbott
14 Oct. 1908
4 Nov. 1997

H522

**Dorothy May
Bishop**
Died 18th September 1983
aged 73 years

H523

John Green
22.11.1910
17.2.1997

———

H524

In loving memory
of
**Barbara Kathleen
Emary**
1908 - 1995

———

H525

**James Michael
Skates**
Died 20th May 1982
aged 51 years

———

H526

Keeley 1996
Liam 1997

———

H527

In loving memory of
**Evelyn Amalie
Baker-Duly**
Born Sept. 1st 1907
Died Oct. 13th 1994

★ Note – **Evelyn Amalie Duly** in Burials Register

———

H528

**Jarvis
Olive G.**
1907 - 1994
George W.
1904 - 1994
Re-united

H529

In memory of
Violet May Laker
8.3.1906 - 18.9.1994
and her husband
Guy William Laker
5.11.1902 - 28.5.1966

H530

**Mary Osmond
Wigg**
Died 3rd July 1994
aged 82

H531

Our much loved son
and brother
David John Leng
Born 12th April 1972
Died 23rd February 1991
Always in our thoughts

H532

**Douglas John
Osborne**
Died 12th August 1990
aged 86 years

H533

**Joyce May
Turner**
Died 27th February 1990
aged 60 years

H534

**Frank Walter
Rigelsford**
Died 16th December 1977
aged 69 years

**Agnes Emily
Rigelsford**
Died 28th June 1984
aged 73 years

H535

**Leonard Hugh
Ryan**
Died 23rd November 1989
aged 92 years

Eileen Mabel Ryan
13.3.1918
1.4.1997
aged 79 years

H536

**Queenie Dorothy
Hamilton-Harris**
Died 27th August 1969
aged 77 years

Claude Hamilton-Harris,
M.C.,
Died 2nd September 1977
aged 89 years

H537

**Robert
Morris**
Died 10th October 1989
aged 76 years

H538

**Violet Ivy
Payne**
Died 13th August 1989
aged 65 years

H539

**James J. T.
Pannett**
Died 27th July 1973
aged 69 years

**Rose Annie
Pannett**
Died 30th July 1990
aged 81 years

H540

**Delia Mary
Layland**
Died 26th October 1972
aged 63 years

H541

**Dennis Drewell
Sisson**
Died 5th August 1989
aged 72 years

H542

Helena Cain
18.1.1956
Died 12th June
1996

H543

**Trevor
Peace**
Died 8th January 1989
aged 96 years

**Diane Elena
Peace**
Died 19th July 1992
aged 74 years

H544

**Dorothy Phyllis
Roberts**
Died 20th January 1988
aged 73 years

**Alfred James
Roberts**
Died 10th November 1988
aged 78 years

H545

**John Charles
Moore**
Died 15th February 1988
aged 84 years

**Ellen Mary
Moore**
Died 25th September 1989
aged 84 years

H546

In loving
memory of
Dean Poulton
2nd September
1986

MEMORIALS

INSIDE THE CHURCH AND ALSO IN THE CHURCHYARD

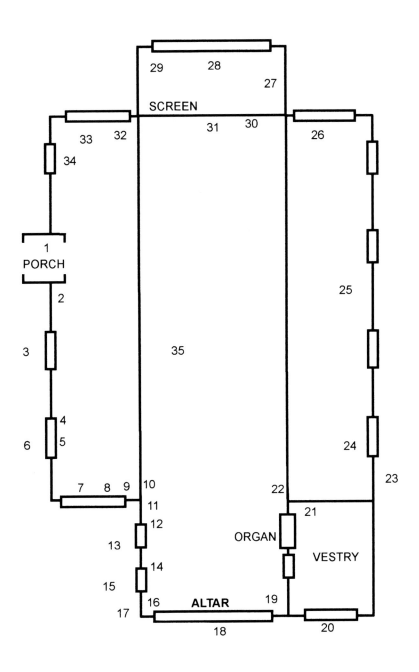

1M

Plaque

This churchyard was levelled in 1960
through the kindness of
Sir Percy Hunting of Old Whyly
who in memory of
his wife **Dorothy**
most generously gave a sum
sufficient for the levelling
and permanent upkeep

2M

Plaque

To the memory of
the **Rev. Harry Harbord** M.A.,
Rector of this Parish 1882 - 1914
who died May 10th 1920 aged 76
and **Ellen Jane**, his wife, who died May 4th 1927, aged 69
A token of the love and gratitude of their children

3M

Stained glass
window

In loving memory of
Charles Lucius Brooke
Capt. 7th Dn. Gds. Born 4th May
1852 Died at sea 3rd Decr. 1880

4M

Plaque

To the memory of
Ernest Alexander Jones
Headmaster of East Hoathly
Schools 1896–1930 - Churchwarden &
for fifty years choirmaster and
untiring and beloved friend to
this village 13th May 1868 - 14th April 1946

5M

Display table

In memory of
**Annie Kathleen
Waller Routh**

6M

Stained glass
window

To the Glory of God and in loving memory
of **Caroline**
Sarah Clements died 11th Apl.
1886 aged 53 years

7M

Plaque
under
stained
glass
window

In ever loving memory of **Evelyn Helen Arden** of Hesmonds
East Hoathly, the dearly beloved wife of Lieut Col. Lawrence
C. T. Thompson late 8th the Kings Regt. who died at Brighton
on the 28th April 1894 aged 44 years, after many months of
suffering borne with utmost bravery and resignation
"Blessed are the pure in heart for they shall see God"

8M

Plaque under
stained glass
window

This window and clock in the tower were the gift of the late
Ann Kemp of Spring Lodge in this Parish
A^{o} D^{ni} 1875 Laus Deo

9M

Wall plaque

In loving memory of
Captain Stephen Gordon Harbord, M.C., R.F.A.
who was born at East Hoathly Rectory June 2nd 1890
Killed in action near St. Julien August 14th 1917
and buried at Vlamertinghe
He was in the retreat after Mons and present at the
battles of the Marne, Aisne, Somme and at Messines
Mentioned in despatches
A good soldier of his God and his King - a son, brother
and comrade, loving and beloved, he rests in hope

10M

Lectern

H. T. & S. Clements LAVS DEO
AD 1892

11M

Wall plaque

The **Reverend Thomas Porter**
Rector of this Parish and Ripe in the same county
died Sepr 30th 1794 aged 74 years
Mary his wife (only daughter and heiress
of Christopher Coates Esqr. of Wensley
in the county of York and Mary his wife)
died August 1st 1792 aged 67 years
Five of their children died in their infancy, viz:
Catherine August 22d 1753 aged 3 years
Christopher December 18th 1753 aged 2 days
Thomas March 8th 1760 aged 8 months
Elizabeth January 8th 1761 aged 4 years
Thomas September 14th 1761 aged 10 months

12M

Carved on back of
end Choir Stall

A.M.D.G.
et in memoriam fratris amati
Collett Harbord
ob. Jan. 25 1886 æt 30

13M

Stained glass
window

To the glory of God
and in memory of
Sophia Topham Clements
died 1904

14M*

Marble plaque

Sacred to the memory of
Edward Thomas Kemp Esqre
Late Lieutenant of the 61st Regiment Bengal Native Infantry
(youngest son of General G. R. Kemp of Spring Lodge in this Parish)
who was killed during the Indian Mutiny
Whilst with a very small force
he gallantly attacked a large body of the rebels near Bareilly
on the 16th day of January 1859
in the 26th year of his age
having previously been present at the siege and capture of Delhi in 1858
and at the battle of Nujjufghur in the preceding year
Most deeply regretted

★ Note – The plaqe to Edward Thomas Kemp was executed by E. J. Physick SC. London
N.W

15M

Stained glass
window

To the glory of God and in memory of
Sophia Topham Clements died 1904

16M

Brass bookstand

The gift of **K. A. Oakshott**
Barham House 1921

17M*

Memorial on
outside of west
wall

In memory
of **Samuel Atkins**
who served his Grace the Duke of
Newcastle 25 years as gardener and
housekeeper at Halland
He died October 24th A.D. 1742
Etat Suæ 59
Also of **Samuel** son of Samuel Atkins and Hannah his wife
who died March 29th 1728
aged 9 months
Likewise of **Hannah** wife of
Samuel Atkins who died
May 5th 1769 aged 79 years

★ Note – From an old print it is possible to see that this memorial to Samuel Atkins was originally on the east wall of the church. It was placed in its present position when the church was rebuilt.

18M

Stained glass
window

To the glory of God and in loving memory of
Charles Stuart Rickett, M.A.

19M

Plaque beside
mosaics

To the glory of God, and in memory
of the **Rev. Frederick Borrodaile**
of Hesmonds, in this parish who died
5th March 1876 aged 77 and of **Demetria**
his wife, who died 1st May 1885, aged 84
The east wall of this chancel was decorated
in mosaic by their children

20M

Memorial over
door to vestry on
outside wall

This vestry was erected in memory of
Captain Henry Topham Clements
by his fellow parishioners and friends
as a token of regard and appreciation
of his many services to East Hoathly
1901

21M*

Beside the organ

Loop System for the Deaf
Given in loving memory of
Frederick Matthew Lockwood
1887 - 1978
and
Beatrice Elizabeth Lockwood
1881 - 1971

★ Note - this plaque is not visible to the public

22M

Pulpit

To the glory of God
and in loving memory of the
Revd. Edward Langdale 54 years
Rector of this Parish
This pulpit is erected by his children
Anno Domini 1892

23M

Stained glass
window

Sacred in ever loving memory
of **Sophia Clements** died
23rd July 1904 aged 66 years

For God For King For Country

To the glorious memory of
the men of
East Hoathly
who gave their lives for
our Empire.
In the Great War 1914-1918

And 1939-1945

Service Personnel

D. J. Drake
J. Goodhart
R. A. Hunting
C. Quested
A. Somerset
T. Tomlinson
V. Turner

Civilians

Mrs. C. A. Goodhart
Master M. J. Goodhart
Mrs. A. M. Smith
Miss C. Somerset

L. Ellis
A. J. Bishop
W. W. Woodhams
C. J. Kemp
H. Corke
A. G. Hutson
P. S. C. Jones
H. M. Piper
A. A. Brooker
G. T. Goldsmith
W. G. Carley
G. E. H. Peskett
R. Burgess
R. W. Beal
S. G. Harbord
D. Russell
E. N. Hurd
E. Morley
W. G. Kemp
C. J. Colbran

*Greater love hath no man than this that
a man lay down his life for his friends*

Stained glass
window

To the glory of God and in memory of **Joseph Rickett** of
Barham House, East Hoathly Born 1819 died 1892

183

26M*

Elaborate
memorial
in bell tower

To the memory of **John Mittell**, Esq.,
of the Moat in this Parish who died 12th Nov. 1734 aged 63
He was active and vigilant in business
and a very usefull member of society
To the memory likewise of **Martha**
wife of the above John Mittell who died 5th July 1738 aged 73
This monument is erected
in gratitude to the best of parents
by their only daughter
Elizabeth Brown

★ Note – This memorial was executed by Edwd Peirce, Dept Ford Kent

---

27M

Stained glass
window

To the Glory of God and in memory
of a beloved mother **Catherine Harbord**
died Oct. 24 1892 aged 82

28M

Carved screen
between nave
and tower

1901
To the Glory
of God and in
loving memory of
**Henry Topham
Clements**

29M

Ledger in front of
door to tower

Here lieth interred the body of

John Mittell, Esq. late of ^e_y
Moate in this Parish who died
November 12th 1734
aged 63 years

184

30M*

```
                    H. S. C.

    TH

    H

                                    ANO
                                  DOMINO
                                    1  92
```

★ Note – This is a very worn ledger in the bell ringing room. There is also a carved Victorian screen placed over a portion of it, but the above letters and numbers are just discernable. The Parish Burial Register records that the Revd. Timothy Parker, Rector, was buried on November 11th 1692. As the ledger for the Rev. Haworth was removed from this same room during building work, I think it is most likely this is the ledger for the Revd. Parker. H.S.C. are the initials for Hic Sepultus Corpus – Here is buried the body.

31M

The windows in the
Gables of the nave
and aisle were
inserted A.D. 1895
in loving memory
of **Evelyn Helen Arden Thompson**
by her husband

32M

Plaque on pew
under stained glass
window

To the glory of God and the memory of **Joseph Rickett** of
Barham House, East Hoathly Born 1819 Died 1892

33M

To the glory of God and the beloved memory of
Cordelia J. Rickett of Barham House, East Hoathly
Born 1826; died 1896

34M*

Metal plaque
(from the coffin)
on side of pew

Christ. Coates Porter
Esq.
Died 6th Feb. 1811
aged 5

* Note – There is a brick vault under the central aisle where the lead coffin for Christopher
Coates Porter lies.

35M

Lych Gate

To God's glory, & in memory of **Edward Langdale, B.A.,** 54 years Rector of this Parish
"My flesh shall rest in hope"
Erected by his parishioners & friends 1883
"Be ye also ready"

36M

War memorial
by entrance gate

R. W. Beal	E. N. Hurd
A. J. Bishop	A. G. Hutson
A. A. Brooker	P. S. C. Jones
R. Burgess	C. J. Kemp
W. G. Carley	W. G. Kemp
C. J. Colbran	E. Morley
H. Corke	G. E. H. Peskett
L. Ellis	H. M. Piper
G. T. Goldsmith	D. Russell
S. G. Harbord	W. W. Woodhams

To the Glory of God and to the gallant memory of
the men of East Hoathly
who fell fighting for King and Country in the Great War 1914-1918
Their names are recorded above
1939 – 1945
Service Personnel

D. J. Drake	J. Goodhart
R. A. Hunting	C. Quested
A. Somerset	T. Tomlinson

V. Turner
Civilians
Mrs. C. A. Goodhart
Master M. J. Goodhart

Mrs. A. M. Smith	Miss C. Somerset

G37M

Seat outside front
porch

In memory of
Diane and Trevor Peace

H38M

Seat

In loving memory of **David John Leng**

H39M

Seat

In memory of our daddy
Philip John Akehurst
25th Nov. 1956 – 13th March 1995

E40M

Inset in church
wall

P. D.
Aeprill 24
1648

G41M

Brass plaque on
churchyard gate

The churchyard gates were repaired
And replaced where necessary in 1960
In memory of **Rosamund Ann McIntosh**
Died 3rd Oct. 1957

POTTED HISTORIES

E182 - Thomas Turner and his family

Throughout the first of these obituaries the name of Thomas Turner will occur. He was shop-keeper, undertaker, schoolmaster, tax-gatherer and churchwarden, and he kept a diary between the years 1754-1765 which provides a great deal of information about the village and its inhabitants.

Thomas Turner was the head of the East Hoathly family. He originally lived in Framfield, but came to East Hoathly in 1750 when he took over the premises of Francis Weller who had died in 1748. Thomas married Margaret, "Peggy", Slater in 1753 and Mary Hicks in 1765. A comprehensive family tree is given in the book "The Diary of Thomas Turner", edited by David Vaisey.

Thomas Turner noted all the funerals in his diary. These included three of the Porter children. On Monday the 14th September 1761 he had a particularly busy day, when he went to screw down the coffin of Thomas Porter, the Rev. Porter's 10 month old son; he then went to serve at the funeral of John French, aged 17; back to the Porters and attended Church, met John French's corpse and attended that funeral, and arrived home at 6.45 in the evening.

At all the funerals mentioned Thomas Turner supplied all the favours, gloves for men, women and children and the hat bands.

At the funeral of Richard Marchant on Sunday 22nd May 1757 Turner did not entirely approve of the sermon, feeling "...it to be a sermon made before the death of Master Marchant".

G260 - Jeremiah and John French

The French family are another East Hoathly family to be well documented by Thomas Turner in his diary. Jeremiah was the tenant farmer of Whyly; he was a dominant character in the area and in noting his death Thomas Turner says he died "after a long and lingering illness, which, it's to be doubted, was first brought on by the too frequent use of spirituous liquors and particularly gin. ... I should think he could not drink less on a moderate computation than 20 gallons a year ..."

John French, Jeremiah's son, had died in 1761 after 6 months illness.

17M - Samuel and Hannah Atkins

Samuel Atkins was steward and gardener to the Duke of Newcastle at Halland House Samuel had left the interest on £100 to be distributed to the poor of East Hoathly and Thomas Turner in his Diary notes on Sunday 7th February 1762 that "...After churchtime Mr. French, Jos. Fuller and myself gave away among the poor of this parish the £41 received yesterday of Mr. Porter and John Piper, it being the interest money of a hundred pounds left by Mr. Sam. Atkins to this parish, for-ever, the interest of which is yearly to be distributed among the poor of this parish in such man-ner and to such persons as the minister and churchwarden for the time being shall think proper..."

The following year he again gave away £4 interest amongst 27 people, but the amount given was in excess of the £4 so Mr. Porter made up the difference from money given at the sacrament. The legacy was subsumed into the general Parish funds after the church was repaired in the 1760s.

Hannah, Samuel's widow, was part of the group which included Turner who went to all the parties and social gatherings which took place in the first two months of each year.

F214 - Joseph Burgess

Joseph Burgess was a farmer, an alehousekeeper and victualler. He kept the Maypole, which later became the Kings Head and is another inhabitant of the village who featured in Thomas Turner's diary.

F222 - Thomas Davy

Thomas Davy, shoemaker, was Thomas Turner's best friend. Turner was shocked when Davy married the Widow Virgo rather unexpectedly, not inviting Turner to the wedding. He was even more shocked when a baby was born 6 months after the wedding "...two people whom I should the least have suspected of being guilty of so indiscreet an act ..."

14M - Lieutenant Edward Thomas Kemp

On Tuesday 25th January 1859 General Kemp gave a ball and supper at Spring Lodge to which most of the "*élite* of the parish" and a good many of the leading families of the neighbourhood had been invited. "The supper was most *recherché* " and there was dancing until nearly 5 o'clock. Unfortunately, General Kemp and his wife were unaware that their youngest son, Lieutenant Edward Thomas Kemp, had been killed on Wednesday the 16th January. Such were the communications in 1859 that it appears they did not hear of his death until the beginning of March, the report appearing in the issue of the local paper of the 15th March.

It was the time of the Indian Mutiny, and Lieutenant Kemp and his men had been instructed to intercept a large group of rebel sepoys who were endeavouring to cross a ford, and so escape into the Rohilcund district. They were successful in driving back the enemy, but in so doing both officers and one third of the men were shot and sabred. Lieutenant Kemp was shot through the body, lingering until the next day, although he appeared free of pain. He was 26 years old.

General Kemp died on the 16th September 1861.

The Holman Family, Surgeons

In the 1800s there were two separate Holman families in East Hoathly; the Farming and Milling Holmans, and the Surgeon Holmans.

In 1816 Henry Holman came to live in East Hoathly with his uncle, Robert Colgate, who was a surgeon. In 1827 Henry married Mary Turner, daughter of Philip and granddaughter of Thomas Turner. They had 9 children, three of whom were given the second name of Colgate, and one child the second name of Martin, Mary's mother's maiden name.

In 1876 it is noted in the Post Office Directory that Henry Holman and Sons were surgeons in the village; that is Thomas living at the Gatehouse and Henry Colgate living at Lydfords. Henry senior was living at Park Lodge.

F209 - Matthew Colman

I have been unable to discover where Matthew Colman worked. From the census returns (1851–1881) he was unmarried and lodged with the Bristow family. Perhaps he worked for one of the large houses and it was his employers who arranged the inscription on his gravestone.

E191 - Henry and Alfred Russell

On the morning of Sunday the 11th June 1876 thousands of people thronged the beaches of Eastbourne to watch the attempted rescue of 12 young men and one child from the sea after their hired fishing lugger, the Nancy's Pride, had capsized. The vessel had been sailing for a short while, when there was a lull in the wind, then there was a great gust which caused water to be shipped in, the entire party rushed to one side of the craft causing it to capsize, throwing everyone into the sea.

The coastguard galley and several fishing vessels set sail immediately to help, but found only one survivor clinging to an oar. Henry and Alfred drowned with the rest of the party. An inquest was held and Henry Russell, their father, said that his two sons had only lately gone to live in Eastbourne, neither of them could swim and he had "never known them go into the water."

G289 and A74 - The Rickett Family

Joseph Rickett of Barham was of the firm of Rickett, Smith & Co., Coal merchants. In 1883 Joseph's youngest son, Charles Stuart, died at the age of 26 from acute pneumonia. He had been educated at Eastbourne College and Christ's College, Cambridge and obtained a degree with honours.

In 1892 Joseph died, leaving a personal estate of upwards of £307,000. At the church service on the Sunday after the funeral, the Rev. Harbord made reference to the great contribution he had made to the village, being a churchwarden and also a Manager of the Schools. He had been brought up in Lolham Mills, Northants, went to London in 1828 and eventually became the senior partner in the firm of Rickett, Smith & Co., coal merchants. "He took a leading part in the revolution in the coal trade, effected by the introduction of the Yorkshire and Midland Coal into London by railway, and was one of the first to take advantage of the new development".

Because of poor health he had spent the last twenty years of his life in the cultivation and management of his estate. "His genial and kindly disposition endeared him to all."

G265 - Henry Topham Clements and Family

Captain Clements, who lived at Belmont, died after an accident at Buxton where he was on holiday. He caught his foot in a kerb stone, injuring his spine, and this injury proved fatal. One report suggests he sustained a broken neck.

Captain Clements and his first wife, Caroline Sarah, had 5 children, two children dying in infancy. Caroline died aged 53 in 1886 and in 1887 he married Sophia Borrodaile, who was living with her parents at Hesmonds. This was a popular marriage - when the couple arrived back in the flag-decorated village after their honeymoon, they were met by the villagers and as the local press reported "...Immediately on the arrival of the carriage at Park Lodge the horse was quickly removed and strong arms quickly conveyed the wedding party to Belmont amidst the lusty cheers of the spectators. Loud reports announced that the blacksmiths had fired their anvils while the bells from the tower rang out a joyous peal."

Captain Clements' death left the village without its greatest benefactor. He had a tremendous interest in the well-being of the village and its inhabitants. It was he who arranged the fund raising and the building of the village school; he saw to the smooth running of its affairs and was very proud that it was the best in the diocese; he was churchwarden for 34 years; and he was a magistrate and also sat on many committees.

Sophia died in 1904.

E200 - George W. C. Ranger

This young man "of much promise" died suddenly aged 18 of consumption. There was a large number of friends and acquaintances, including the children of the Sunday School, at the funeral. George's grandfather aged 93 was also there; he died 2 years later.

George's father was Peter Ranger, the owner of the East Hoathly general stores.

E192 - Minnie Jane Woodhams

From the local paper of the 25th August 1882 -

SUDDEN DEATH

On Tuesday morning a child named Minnie J. Woodham age 2 years and 7 months, daughter of a miller residing in High Street was taken ill. Dr. Holman was sent for and prescribed but the child got rapidly worse and died in the evening. A medical certificate of the cause of death having been given the Coroner considers an inquest unnecessary.

G266, G292, G293 - The Harbord Family

The Rev. Harry Harbord came to East Hoathly in 1882, he married and had 9 children, one dying when only 3 days old. He died whilst out riding in Park-street, Horsham. His servant, who was driving a horse and trap a short way behind, saw him put both hands up to his chest and then he fell from the saddle, apparently having died immediately.

Captain Stephen Gordon Harbord, M.C. was the sixth child of the Rev. Harbord. He was killed in France by a splinter from an enemy shell. Before the outbreak of war he was on the special reserve of officers, and at the commencement of war he was commissioned to the R.F.A. in France. After a period of sick leave in 1915 he joined the artillery of an Ulster Division and it was then he was awarded his MC.

E190- Rev. C. Ridley Richardson

Christopher Ridley Richardson had a very crowded and varied life. He had been fruit farming in Canada when he returned to England at the commencement of the First World War. He joined the Army, reaching rank of Captain, then transferred to the Royal Flying Corps and continued in the R.A.F. until 1927. During this time he was seconded to the Royal Navy. He was ordained in 1930 and rejoined the R.A.F. in 1934 as padre, serving for nine years, four of which were in Malta.

He took a great interest in local affairs, including the British Legion, and he was also chairman of the managers of the school.

Upon his retirement in 1961 he and his wife moved to Seaford.

A6 - William Parris

William Parris was the owner of the Providence Chapel in East Hoathly. He had been born in East Hoathly, but had started a bakery business in Brighton in about 1890, returning to East Hoathly some 30 years later.

E189 - Alfred Davidson Allan

Mr. Allan was born in Adelaide, South Australia and was associated with a firm of merchants and shipowners of Melbourne and London. He moved to Singapore to become Chairman of another firm but in 1916 left to come to England to be the Manager of the London Branch. Whilst he was in Singapore he was a member of the Volunteers and Col. F. J. Agg, of Chiddingly, was his commanding officer. Presumably this is why he settled in East Hoathly at a house called Firgrove (now called Spring Place). Mr. Allan was a keen sportsman and he took a great interest in local affairs becoming involved in the Football Club, the Carnival Society and he was a manager of the School. He and his wife provided the annual Christmas tree and tea for the schoolchildren. He had been married only six years at the time of his death.

G299 - Peter Starnes and Gordon George Heasman

These two young lads aged 19 were unfortunately killed on the 7th December 1946 when their motorcycle hit a three ton lorry at Wych Cross. The Coronor, at the inquest, said after recording a verdict of Accidental Death, that if there was any fault at all it was through a misunderstanding on the part of the A.A. Scout.

A.A. Scout Anderson said he thought the driver of the lorry, who was turning into the Eastbourne road, had slowed as he had wanted to ask a question; the lorry driver thought that the A.A. Scout was waving him on, and he had reached the middle of the road just as the motorcycles appeared. The unfortunate incident was witnessed by Phillip Starnes who was riding his motor cycle some yards behind his brother and Gordon Heasman.

A1 and A13 - The Jones Family

Frederick and Caroline Jones came to East Hoathly School in 1870 when Frederick was appointed Head Master, a position he held until his retirement in 1890, when they moved to Kirby Cottage, South Street. In 1890 their son Frederick Thomas became headmaster until his death some five years later, when his brother Ernest Alexander was appointed.

In 1911 Thomas Alfred the eldest child of Ernest Alexander Jones was successfully operated on for appendicitis. In November of the same year his daughter Alice Alexandra, known as Cissie, also needed the same operation, but unfortunately she was not so lucky and she died.

B87 - Elizabeth Jane Stokes

It was reported that Miss Stokes aged 75 had been ill for some time, had been unable to get out much during the winter months, but was only ill for two days before her death, "her final illness being both short and painful".

She originally came from Devonshire, but had made her home in East Hoathly to be with her sister and brother-in-law, Mr. and Mrs. J. Turner of Mill House.

G313 - Group Captain Goodhart and family

It was estimated that on the night of Friday January 21st 1944 there were about 90 enemy planes over the south-east of England, 14 of which were brought down. Bombs were dropped in various districts, but there were few fatal casualties and not too much damage.

Unfortunately the house of Group Captain Goodhart at Greywood was demolished by a bomb which dropped in the garden between the house and a summer house and it caused a crater 40 feet deep. The house was destroyed, but the summer house was untouched! The Group Captain, his wife, small son and his mother-in-law were all killed outright. It is curious that the neighbours did not hear the explosion and the first anyone knew of the incident was when the Chief A.R.P. Warden tried to return home and was brought to a halt by the debris from the damaged house strewn across the road. The unfortunate Group Captain had only arrived home on leave a few hours earlier.

H383, H384 and H444 - Sir Percy Hunting and wives

Sir Percy Hunting served in the First World War with the 4th Northumberland Fusiliers and he was knighted in 1960. In 1910 he married Dorothy Edith Birkett from Bexhill and they had two sons, one was lost in active service on H.M.S. Repulse in 1941. Dorothy died in 1958 and two years later Sir Percy married her sister, Evelyn Marion. They lived at Old Whyly.

War Memorial Dead

Private A. Brooker

Private Albert Brooker of the King's Own Light Infantry was killed in action on the 9th April 1917, aged 19, having joined up the previous September. He had been a pupil at the school, a member of the football team and worked as a groom at Barham. His elder brother was also at the Front.

Private G. T. Goldsmith

Private George Thomas Goldsmith of the Sussex Regiment was killed in action on Easter Monday, having been in France for five months only. He had been gardener at Hesmonds for 23 years. He was 39 and left a widow, a daughter and two sons.

Private R. Burgess

Private Burgess of the Royal Fusiliers was killed instantly by a fragment of shell on 7th June 1917. He had joined the Royal Fusiliers on the 7th June 1916 and had by coincidence been in the services for exactly a year. His Commanding Officer wrote that he was a cheerful and willing worker. He was 35 years old and left a wife and child. In civilian life he had been a gardener at Barham House.

HOW TO USE THIS INDEX

The churchyard has been divided into 8 sections- Sections A - H. All gravestones have been given a number with the prefix of the section in which they can be found. Some numbers are followed by either the letter P or A or both. P indicates a plaque which has been added at a later date to a gravestone and A indicates Ashes. Thus the gravestone for George David Beal is No. A44PA - it can be found in Section A, is a plaque on Grave No. 44 denoting either the scattering or burial of ashes.

Any number followed by the letter M indicates a memorial which can be found either in the church or in the grounds, i.e. a seat, the lych gate, etc. - see separate section for Memorials.

Borrodaile	Demetria	19M		Ruth	C127
	Frederick	19M		Sarah	D151
Bradford	Noreen Mary	H513A		Sarah Ann	C136
Brakefield	Alexander	D155	**Bye**	Mary	D163
	Mary	D155			
Brewis	Katharine Maud	A32PA	**Cain**	Helena	H542A
Bristow	Emma	A34	**Carey**	Charles	H345
	Fanny Maria	F208		Eliza	D153
	Jane	F208		George	D153
	Mark	A34		John	D153
Brook	Mercy	E174	**Carley**	Eunice	A53
Brooke	Charles Lucius	3M		George	A53
Brooker	A. A	24M, 36M		Samuel	E198
	Ada Clara	H437		Sarah	E198
	Arthur Henry	H437		Thomas Henry	H365
	Mary Ann	A40		W. G.	24M, 36M
Brooks	Ernest L.	H353		William George	A49
	Harriott J.	H353	**Carr**	Augusta	A81
Brown	Ida Violet May	H386	**Catt**	Liam Michael	H342
	Ronald	H519A	**Cayley**	Susanna	E184
	Samuel Thomas	H386		William	E183
Buckett	Charles David	A50			
	Charles Edward	A50	**Chatfield**	Emma	G258
	Tamar	A50		Louisa	G259
Buckley	Elsie L	B105		Martha Ruth	H369
	William W.	B105		Richard	F203
Burchett	Amy Ethel	A58		Thomas	G258
	Dorothy M.	H492		William Thomas	H369
	Ernest Robert	H347	**Clark(e)**	Jack	H489
	Esther	A58		John	B120
	Freddie	H357		Nicola Helen	H505
	Sylvia Susetta	H347		Rose Emily	B120
Burfield	Emma	G314		Sally	E182
	Frank Henry	G279	**Clay**	Annie Elizabeth	A64
	Nellie	H470	**Clements**	Caroline Mary	G265
	Nelson Edward John	H470		Caroline Sarah	G265, 6M
	Rowland	G314		Edward Lucius Topham	G265
Burges(s)	Charity	F240		H. T. & S.	10M
	Charlotte	F235		Henry Topham	G265, 20M, 28M
	Frances	F217		Sophia	G265, 23M
	John	F240		Sophia Topham	13M, 15M
	Joseph	F214	**Clift**	Emily Bourne	A63
	R.	24M, 36M		William	A63
	Robert	F235	**Clucas**	Ann	H406
	Sarah	F221, F214		Archie Atkinson	H406
Burnell	Emma Elizabeth	G301	**Coates**	Sarah	C144
Burt	Emily	A35	**Cohn**	Annie	B117
	James William	A35		Harold Charles	B117
Burtenshaw	Annie Harriett	H371	**Cole**	Lilian Marian	H435
	John Dunstone	H371	**Colbran**	C. J.	24M, 36M
	Kitty	A79	**Colman**	Matthew	F209
	Sarah Kate	A79	**Copp**	Helen	B121
Burton	Ernest Clement	H409		Richard H.	B121
	George	D151	**Corke**	H.	24M, 36M
	George Henry	C136		Jack Michael	H480
	John	C127		Wilfred Cecil	H367

Hart	Robert Charles	H509
Hart-Cox	Ernest William	H416
	Kathleen Mary	H416
Haworth	Mr.	F228
Haynes	Emily Laura	G319A
	Frederick William	G318A
Ha(i)zelden	Hannah	G310
	Thomas Charles	H424
Heasman	Ada Clara	C124
	Albert Edward	B88
	Emily	B88
	Gordon George	G299
	William	C124
Hellier	William	B95
Helsdon	Michael Robin	D149
Hemsley	Herbert S.	A68P
Hickie	Frederick Corbett	F238
	Margaret Ann	H430
Hicks	M. Eliz.	E175
Hillier	Agnes	H349
	Helen	B107
	Minnie	H349
Hitchcock	Harry William	F242A
	Marjorie Lena	F242A
Hoare	Alfred Percy	H337
Hoath	Edward	A39
	Ernest	A39
Holman	Edith Mary	A12
	Elizabeth	G303
	Francis Edward	E173
	Henry	E172
	Henry Colgate	A12
	Jane Colgate	E171
	Jane Meade	A12
	Mabel Colgate	A12
	Mary	E171, E172
	Samuel	G303
	Susanna Martin	E171
	Sylvia	A23
	Sylvia May	A23
	Thomas	A23
	Walter Cyril	H414
	Wilfred Eastment	E173
	William	E173
Holmes	F. E	A2.
	Richard Allen Compton	G289
	Walter	A2
Howard	Alfred Gravely	H355
	Edith Caroline	H355
	Frank	H336
Humphrey	Melvyn	H490
Hunnard	Harriot	A59
Hunnisett	Albert	H362
	Amy G.	H362
	Emily	G325
	John Pentecost	G307, G325

	Mary	G306
	Mary Jane	H362
	Richard	G306
	Rosina Jessie	G307
Hunt	Caroline	A68
	Caroline Alice	A68
	Christiana Alice	F241
	Ernest Edward	A68
	Robert James	F241
	Walter	A68
Hunting	Dorothy	1M
	Dorothy Edith	H383
	Evelyn Marion	H444
	Percy Llewellyn	H384
	R. A.	24M, 36M
Hurd	Albert Ernest	F232
	E. N.	24M, 36M
	Mary Martha	F232
Hutson	A. G.	24M, 36M
	John Blishen	A52
	Olive	A52
	Percy Blishen	A52
Hylands	Gladys Rosaline	D157
	John Henry William (Jack)	H463
	Lydia	A73P
	Rhoda Betty	H419
Jarvis	George W.	H528A
	Olive G	H528A
Jeffery	Elizabeth Jane	B113
	Elsie Agnes Norah	H469
	Foreman	H469
	Frederick George	B113, H469
	James	H446
	Lily May	H460
	Norah	H469
	William Edward	H460
Jenkins	Glynn Thomas	H485
Jenner	Charles Albert	H410
	Emily Mary	F231
	Winifred	H410
Jobson	Marion Ruby	H448
Johnson	Theodosia	E180
	William	E180
	William Hardy	F202
Jolly	Ian Harry	H465
Jones	Alice Alexandra "Cissie"	A13
	Alice Elizabeth	A1
	Caroline	A13
	Christine Ann	H390
	David Harold	H389
	Doris Evelyn	H389
	Emily Anne	A60
	Ernest Alexander	A1, 4M
	Frederick	A13
	Frederick Thomas	A13

	George	H497
	George David	A21
	Henry	A60
	Leslie	H422
	Mary	A21
	Molly	H422
	Nellie	H497
	P. S. C.	24M, 36M
	Thomas Hugh	H434
Judd	Mildred	F237
	Samuel C.	F237
Keeley	Clifford Robert	H411PA
	Liam	H526A
	Mabel	H411PA
Kemp	Ann	G286, 8M
	C. J.	24M, 36M
	Edward Thomas	14M
	Elizabeth	A11
	Fanny	F234
	George Rees	G286
	John Frederick	H374
	Mary Ann	E185
	Mary Rose	H405
	Walter	A11
	Walter Albert	H405
	W. G.	24M, 36M
	Walter Luther	A25
	William George	A25
Knight	Emily Joyce	G291
	Florence Amy	H449
	Frank	G300
	George	H449
	John Frederick	G321
	Mary Beatrice	G300
	Robert	G291
	Sarah Jane	G321
	Walter Seymour	A55
Laker	Guy William	H529A
	Violet May	H529A
Lambert	George Arrow	H352
	Hilda Mary	H352
Langdale	Ann Lucy	G295
	Caroline Anne	G264
	Charlotte	G294
	Edward	G290, G332, 22M, 35M
	Edward Rudstone	G332
	Elizabeth	G294, G332
	Emily Elizabeth	G332
	Emily Mary	G290
	Henry Marmaduke	A76
	Mary	G295
	Rose Ellen	A76
Langdon	Ellen Fitzherbert	G330
Larking	John	F227

	Mercy	F227
Last	Marjorie Grace	A54A
Lawrence	Liam Michael	H342
Layland	Delia Mary	H540A
Leng	David John	H531A, H38M
Leeson	George	C139
Leigh	Gladys Muriel	H484
Lester	Eliza Kate	C131
	Kate	C131
Lindsay	George William	A49
Littlewood	Eliza	B99
	William	B99
Lockwood	Frederick Matthew	21M
	Beatrice Elizabeth	21M
Loftus St. George	Clifford Fortes	H421
Logan	Rachel Wylie	H502
Lovell	Elizabeth	F213
	Emy	F213
	John	F213
Mackness	Gilbert Thomas	A61
Macrae	Amy	H333
Magub	Douglas	F247A
	Ninette	F247A
Mannering	Bertha Mary	A20
	David	A15
	David Leslie	A20
	Kezia Penelope	A15
	Maude	A20
Maples	Henrietta	G267
Marant	Reginald Ernest	H366
Marchant	George	H338
	Mary	F223
	Richard	F223
	Violet May	H338
Martin	Joanna Kay	H486
Masters	William Stuart	H482
Mathews	Annie	G316
	Charles Henry	G316
	Mary Matilda	G316
	Naomi	G316
McIntosh	Rosamund	F236A, G41M
Meakin	Marion Louise	H520A
Medcalf	Jessie	H402
Miles	Albert Harvey	H481
	Joan Evelyn	H481
Mitchell	Anthony Steven	H403
	Edith Augusta	G322
	Emily	H387
	Frank	H387
	Fred	H415
	Nellie	H415
	Tony	H403
Mittell	John	26M, 29M
	Martha	26M
Moore	Elizabeth	B115

	Ellen Mary	H545A		Rebecca	G311
	John Charles	H545A		Robert	A45
	Nellie	H346		Sarah	A45, G310
	Timothy	B115		Sarah Ann	G309
Morley	Caroline Laura	A51		William	A6
	Charles	H432	**Partridge**	James	A33
	E.	24M, 36M		Lilian Mary	A33
	Isabel Violet	B98		William	A33
	Ronnie (Laddie)	A48	**Payne**	Violet Ivy	H538A
Morris	MorleyWilliam	A51	**Peace**	Diane	G37M
	Robert	H537A		Diane Elena	H543A
Morton	Caroline	F210		Dora Annie	H423
Mullard	Mary	B100		Trevor	H543A, G37M
	Mary Eliza	B100	**Pearson**	Harold William	H356
	Thomas	B100	**Pelham**	Kate Wheeler	G270
Mylius	Frances Rosella Mary	G308	**Peskett**	Arthur William Chalmers	A8
				Edith Jane	A8
Newman	Joseph William	H476		Enid Blanche	A8
	Sarah	H476		G. E. H.	A8, 24M, 36M
Nicholls	Frank	H445	**Pettit**	Ada Mary	H428
Norman	Ann	G282		Bernard Arthur	H428
	Hannah	D154		Eric Harold	H467
	Henry	D154		Kathleen Florence	H467
	Sarah Jane	G275	**Phillips**	Leonard Harry	F250A
Novis	Ann	A14	**Piper**	H. M.	24M, 36M
	Edward Thomas	H350	**Pitman**	Arthur Edward	H483
	Harriett Maud	H350	**Playne**	Alfred Henry	B93
	Lucy	A84		Anne E.	B93
	Samuel	A84		Edith Mary	H380
	Thomas	A14		Mildred Lucetta	H380
			Porter	Catherine	11M
Oakshott	K. A.	16M		Christ. Coates	34M
Oliver	Leonard William	H504		Christopher	11M
Osborne	Douglas John	H532A		Elizabeth	11M
Ovenden	Annie Amelia	H443		John C.	H450
	Thomas Frank	H443		Mary	11M
				Thomas	11M
Page	Kate	E190	**Poulton**	Dean	H546A
Paine	David	F239	**Prescott**	Constance	H379P
	John	G274	**Press**	Eleanor Julia	H391
	Mary	G274			
	Nathaniel	G274	**Quested**	Connell	H339, 24M, 36M
	Susanna	F239		George	H339
Palmer	Cicely Margaret	H385		Kate	H339
Pankhurst	Ann	C134			
	Ernest A.	G297	**Radley**	Arthur	H392
	George	C134	**Ralph**	George	A18
	John	C137		Harriett	A18
Pannett	James J. T.	H539A	**Ranger**	Catherine M.	G302
	Rose Annie	H539A		Charles P.	G302
Parker	Timothy	30M		George William Carey	E196
Parris	Edmund	A9, G309		Loanna Mary	E196
	Edward	A82, G311		Peter	E196
	Hannah	A6, A9	**Raynes**	Edward	F229
	John	G311	**Reed**	John Henry	A7
	Mary Ann	A82		Sarah	A7

Rich	Andrew Francis	A47			Mary	B111
	Elizabeth	C145, E200	**Shanks**	John James	H471
	Emily Minnie	A37	**Shorter**	Caroline	A21
	Ernest Robert	H378A	**Sims**	Henry James	E192
	Florence Minnie	H378	**Sinden**	George	H496
	Frances	C145	**Sisson**	Dennis Drewell	H541A
	George	C145	**Skates**	James Michael	H525A
	Henry	C142, C143, C145	**Smith**	Alice Maud	G313, 24M, 36M
	Jane	C139		Arthur Sydney	F252A
	Maria Ann	A47		Elizabeth	A83, G281
	Mary	E199		George	A83
	Mary Ann	C146		Joan	H503
	Robert Walter	H378A		Josias	G281
	Sarah	C143		Lilian Mary	F252A
	Sarah Jane	C145	**Snodgrass**	Janet	E176
	Thomas	C139	**Somerset**	A.	24M, 36M
	William Andrew	A37		C.	24M, 36M
Richards	George Charles	H466		Henrietta	H395
Richardson	Christopher Ridley	E187		John	H395
	Gwyneth Mary	E187	**Spaull**	Sydney Maurice	F251A
	Rose Matilda	B110P	**Spencer**	Elizabeth Lilian	H417
Rickett	Charles Stuart	G289, 18M	**Spooner**	John	E190
	Cordelia	A74	**Starnes**	Emily	H370
	Cordelia Jane	G289, 33M		Frederick	H370
	Joseph	G289, 25M, 32M		Jane	D156
Rigelsford	Agnes Emily	H534A		Peter Richard	G299
	Frank Walter	H534A		Samuel	D156
Roberts	Alfred James	H544A	**Starr**	Kathleen Mary	H379
	Dorothy Phyllis	H544A	**Steel**	Eva Minnie	H399
Robinson	Elizabeth	G296		Harriett Rebecca	H400
	Henry	G296		Harry	H399
	Sarah Emily	H358		Hazel Patricia "Pat"	H400P
Roffey	Beatrice May	H463		William Henry Thomas	H398
	Frank A.	A75	**Stepney**	Charles	H368
Rogers	George	A72		Lucy	B118
	George Arnold	A72		Minnie	H368
Routh	Annie Kathleen Waller	H518A, 5M		Richard	B118
Rushton	Mary Edith	F238	**Stevens**	Audrey Margaret	H478
Russell	Alfred	E188		Hilda May	B91PA
	Arthur	F219		Rodney St. Vincent	B91
	Charles	F215, F220	**Stewart**	Alexander	A30
	D.	24M, 36M		Cordelia	G289
	Henry	E188		Donald	F248A
	Jane	F220		Eleanor Ninette	F248A
	Mary Noakes	F215		Jean	A30PA
Ryan	Eileen Mabel	H535A		Ruby May	F249A
	Leonard Hugh	H535A	**Stickland**	Louisa	A19
			Stokes	Elizabeth Jane	B87
Salter	Ray	H452	**Streeter**	Edward	A32
Saunders	Catherine	A62		Eliza Kate	A16
	Ethel Annie	H413		Lilian Maude	A16
	George	A62		Mary	A70
	Gilbert Thomas	H413		Sarah Jane	A32
	Isabel May	E197		Thomas	A70
	Thomas	H413	**Strong**	Charles	H517A
Seymour	George	B111	**Sutton**	Catherine	H333P

Swann — Frances Evelyn — G266
Terry — Hannah — G276
William — G276
Thatcher — Louisa — A66
Thomas — Marion Frances — H343
Thompsett — Jim — H479
Thompson — Eliza Story — F256A
Evelyn Helen Arden — 7M, 31M
John William — F256A
Thomson — Helen Kate — H373
Thorpe — Daisy May — C128PA
Emma — C128
Olive Maude — H515A
Philip James — H515A
Sampson B. — C128
Thurgood — Julia — H351
Tilly — Hannah — D165
Walter Fuller — D165
Tomlinson — T. — 24M, 36M
Trill — Alfred — C148
Alice Ann — H381
Blanche — A28P
David William — A31
Edith Mary — C147
George Henry — A27
George Reginald — A28
Harriet Ruth — A31
Herbert — C147
Julia — A27
Mary — C148
Reginald — A28P
Samuel Holford — H381
Trussler — Harry George — G326
Mary Louisa — G326
Turner — Albert Edward — C138
Alice Kate — C125
Audrey Batley — E177
Charlotte — B103, B95P
Charlotte Martin — E177
Clara Shaw — C138
Edith — H359
Emily Mary — B112
Emma — B101
Frederick — B103, E179
John — B101, C140
John Percy — B102
Joyce May — H533A
Lillie — F254A
Margaret — E178
Martha — C140, D162
Mary — H360
Mary Ann — H341
Michael — E177
Peter — E179
Philip — E177
Phoebe — A66P

Reginald Frederick — H359
Robert — D162
Sarah — E177
Sarah Martin — E177
Sidney Charles — H360
Stanley — H341
Stephen Martin — E177
Susanna Martin — E177
Thomas — E178
V. — 24M, 36M
William — B95P
William Wallace — F254A
Veners — Edwin — G320
Venner — Elsie Martha — H354
John Frank — H354
Verrall — Gladys Frances May — H506
Vine — Ann — D170
Wain — Kate — F205
Walker — Horace Radcliffe — E191
Louisa Patience — E191
Walls — Susan — D170
Thomas — D170
Walter — Fanny — A79
Warren — William — F207
Watford — Barbara — G285
Ellen — G285, G304
Frederick — G284
George — G285
Jemima — G283
Mary — G304
Samuel — G283
Watkins — Muriel Dorothy — H487
Webb — Elizabeth Ruth — B110
John — B110
Weller — Rebecca — F216
Ann — F211
Francis — F216
Mary — F211
Rebekah — F211
Wenham — Edith Martha — A57
Ernest George — H494
Ethel Rhoda — H453
Mary — A46
Rhoda — A57
William — A46
West — Edith — H455
Westgate — Alice — C126
Annie — C132, H348
Frederick Thomas — C126
George — H348
Harriet — H348
Walter — H348
Whapham — Margaret — A43
Wickerson — Elizabeth — F204

Military

4th Middlesex Regiment	A49	Pilot	E187
7th Dragoon Guards Captain	3M	Pilot Officer	H399
13th and 14th KingsLight Dragoons, Captain	G265	R.A. Captain	F244
22nd Regiment Bombay Native Infantry, Colonel	G286	R.A.F.	E187
61st Regiment Bengal Native Infantry, Lieutenant	14M	R.A.F.V.R.	H399
Captain	20M	R.F.A.	9M
Chaplain	E187	Royal Air Force, Group Captain	G313
Her Majesty's Indian Army, General	G286	Royal Canadian Horse Artillery	A49
Indian Army, Lt. Col.	F238	Royal Navy Captain	H481
Indian Army, Major	F252A		

Place Names

Adelaide	E186	Mays, Sussex	G273
Aldershot	A28P	Melbourne, Australia	E186
Australia	E186	Moate	26M, 29M
Barham House	16M, 25M, 32M, 33M, G296	Norfolk	E197
Belfast	H477	North Devon	G287
Belmont	F229, G265		
Bolton, Lancs.	B100	Old Possingworth, Waldron	D159, D160
Brighton	G330, H349	Old Whyly	1M, H383, H384, H444
Brockhampton Gloucs.	F205	Ormskirk	H406
Burma	H339		
		Pau-Basses, Pyrenees	E171
Canada	H357	Queensland	G317
Chiddingly	B96P, G331		
Crouch's Farm	A11, A25	Renfrewshire	E176
		Ripe	11M
Eastbourne	D165, E186, E188		
		Simla, India	A8
Fir Grove [Spring Lodge]	8M, 14M, E186, G286	Singapore	E186
Framfield	E198	Southleigh	G291
		Spring Lodge [Firgrove]	8M, 14M, E186, G286
Graywood	H432	Stoke	F210
		Suffolk	D163
Halland	A8, A15, A77, C136, D151, G288, G316		
Halland [House]	17M	Tenterden, Kent	F218
Handforth, Cheshire	B92	Tonbridge	A21
Heathfield	F213		
Hesmonds	7M, 19M	Uffculme, Devon	B95
Hesmonds Farm	A26		
Hove, Sussex,	A21	Waldron	E180, G273
		Wandsworth	G310
India	A32P, B109	Wensley, York	11M
		Westfield , Sussex	G296
Laughton	D161	Westminster, London, S.W.1	A77
Lewes	E194	Whitesmith	B96P
		Wilmington	E175

Occupations

Artist	H440	Minister	A21, G316
Barrister	A21	Missionary nurse	A32P
Blacksmith	B103	Organist	F251A
Carrier	A34	Police Constable	B100
Choir conductor	E187	Postman	B96P
Choir master	4M	Priest	F202
Churchwarden	4M	Rector	2M, 11M, 22M, 30M, 35M, E187, F201,
Draper	E178		F228, G290, G291, G293, G332
Gardener	17M	Spinster	F204
H.M. Customs	G287	Surgeon	A23, E172 , G274
Headmaster	4M, A1, A13	Tallow Chandler	F206
Housekeeper	17M	Vicar	G296
Mercer	E177, F216	Victualler	F240

208

APPENDIX

Because of a delay in the printing of this book, it has been possible to include the following. These have been given the prefix X, and a description of where they are to be found. The numbers are not shown on any of the maps.

X1

Headstone

Section H
between H424 and H425

Clara Hazelden
Died 14th May 1999
Aged 92 years

X2

Inset slab with
Winnie the Pooh
holding balloons

Section H
next to H492

**Charlotte Ivy
Hill**
21.6.96–23.6.96
A special daughter
and sister
Forever in our hearts

X2

Wooden cross
with metal plaque

Section H
next to H510

**Basil Guy
Wintle**
Died 6th June 1999
aged 52 years

X3A

Section H
Garden of Remembrance

In loving memory
Dorothy Frosdick
August 9th 1931
Died December 12th 1998
Isaiah 49 Vs 15

X4A

Section H
Garden of Remembrance

In loving memory
of
Gerry Hilton
19/11/28–11/2/99

Other publications by

CTR Publishing

9 High Street,
East Hoathly,
Nr. Lewes,
East Sussex,
BN8 6DR

THE DIARY OF THOMAS TURNER
1754 – 1765
Edited by David Vaisey

This book is a unique record of life in a rural Georgian village, detailing Thomas Turner's everyday dealings with the inhabitants of East Hoathly. He was shop-keeper, undertaker, schoolmaster, tax-gatherer, churchwarden, overseer of the poor and much more. He tells of his family life, his diet (mostly "leftovers from yester-day"), parties, cricket matches, births, marriages and deaths.

This book is a must for the student of Georgian village life, and also for those researching their East Hoathly ancestors.

Illustrated
386 pages
Price: £8.99 plus £2.70 p&p
From Jane Seabrook, CTR Publishing, 9 High Street, East Hoathly, East Sussex, BN8 6DR

AS CLEAN A LOT OF CHILDREN
AS HE HAD EVER SEEN
Edited by Jane Seabrook

This book tells the story of the building of the East Hoathly schools in 1865, the teaching methods, the punishments, the treats to celebrate national and local events and it tells of the visitors who had nothing but praise for the standards set. It is a revealing document telling of the poverty, epidemics, and the constant struggle to educate children against all the odds.

The information has been edited from the log books from 1865 until a short while after the first World War.

Illustrated with photographs and line drawings by local schoolchildren.
124 pages
Price: £7.95 plus £1.75 p&p
From Jane Seabrook, CTR Publishing, 9 High Street, East Hoathly, East Sussex, BN8 6DR